12/04

Childmate

A Guide to Appraising Quality in Child Care

Join us on the web at

EarlyChildEd.delmar.com

Childmate

A Guide to Appraising Quality in Child Care

Angela Capone, Ph.D.
Southwest Human Development

Tom Oren, Ph.D.
Western Carolina University

John T. Neisworth, Ph.D.
Penn State University

THOMSON

DELMAR LEARNING

Australia   Canada   Mexico   Singapore   Spain   United Kingdom   United States

THOMSON

DELMAR LEARNING

Childmate
A Guide to Appraising Quality in Child Care

Angela Capone, Ph.D.; Tom Oren, Ph.D.; and John T. Neisworth, Ph.D.

Vice President, Career Education SBU:
Dawn Gerrain

Director of Editorial:
Sherry Gomoll

Acquisitions Editor:
Erin O'Connor

Developmental Editor:
Patricia Gillivan

Editorial Assistant:
Ivy Ip

Director of Production:
Wendy A. Troeger

Production Editor:
Joy Kocsis

Technology Project Manager:
Joseph Saba

Director of Marketing:
Donna J. Lewis

Channel Manager:
Nigar Hale

Cover Design:
Joseph Villanova

Composition:
Stratford Publishing Services

For permission to use material from the text or product, contact us by

Tel   (800) 730-2214
Fax   (800) 730-2215
www.thomsonrights.com

Library of Congress Cataloging-in-Publication Data

Capone, Angela.
   Childmate: a guide to appraising quality in child care / Angela Capone, Tom Oren, John T. Neisworth
      p. cm.
Includes bibliographical references and index.
   ISBN 1-40181-622-3
   1. Child care—Handbooks, manuals, etc.   2. Child care—Evaluation.   I. Oren, Tom.   II. Neisworth, John T.   III. Title
   HQ778.5 C367 2003
   649'.1—dc21   20020411284

Contents

Preface

Make no mistake about it; the qualities of the child's circumstances and experiences are critical to healthy, happy, hopeful futures. Development is the result of the constant interplay of biological and environmental circumstances. Of course, caregivers are not in charge of the child's biology, but they are able to offer high-quality experiences for children that can optimize development. While caregivers cannot do much to change a child's biological condition, they can greatly influence development by providing excellent environments and experiences. Good environments and responsive care can change a child's developmental destiny.

Childmate: A Guide to Appraising Quality in Child Care was developed to assist caregivers plan and provide quality services for young children and families. *Childmate* checklists provide a way to consider key environmental aspects. By incorporating the suggestions outlined in each section, you can create a program that is responsive to the needs of children in different stages of development.

What Is Included in *Childmate*?

The information included in *Childmate* represents a synthesis of our current knowledge of quality early care and education environments. Recognizing that development is an interactive process, *Childmate* emphasizes:

- establishing meaningful partnerships with parents
- family culture and traditions as the context of early development
- quality relationships that are key to quality caregiving
- child-centered approaches
- individualized learning experience
- learning through play

Childmate is divided into three sections: "Infancy" (2 to 12 months), "Toddlerhood" (12 to 36 months), and "The Preschool Years" (36 to 60 months). There are four components to each developmental section:

1. Developmental Overview of the Period
2. Guiding Principles for Supporting Optimal Development in Group Care Settings
3. Three checklists: Caregiver Behaviors; Toys and Materials; and Physical Attributes of the Environment
4. Do's and Don'ts

The four components combined provide detailed information for creating a quality early childhood experience for each age group.

Overview of the Developmental Period

Unlike most discussions of child development, which focus on developmental milestones, we present a discussion highlighting two or three themes that summarize the major accomplishments of each development stage. For example, a major accomplishment for infants is human connectedness. These themes or major accomplishments go beyond simple developmental measures that focus on isolated skills (e.g., grasping an object). Instead, the themes focus on the kinds of experiences that are critical to healthy emotional and intellectual growth at each stage of development. Caregivers who are sensitive to these development themes can use them to guide their decision making.

Guiding Principles

The Guiding Principles for Supporting Optimal Development in Group Care Settings expand the discussion of major accomplishments by presenting critical information about how children learn in each developmental stage. Infants, for example, learn primarily through action. Their sensory and motor systems are the primary systems for experiencing and processing the world around them. Preschoolers, on the other hand, are capable of fairly complex thought and behavior. Although preschoolers are still very much on the move, they also experience and process the world through their ability to engage in representational thinking. The principles discussed in this section of *Childmate* will help caregivers to provide learning opportunities for children that match the learning processes at their stage of development.

Checklists

Researchers and practitioners have identified three factors that influence a child's ability to construct and understand his or her world: adult behaviors, toys and materials, and environmental design. *Childmate* includes a checklist for each of these factors for each of the developmental periods.

Caregiver Behaviors: This checklist identifies caregiver behaviors that support optimal development. Items identify activities and behaviors that research and professional opinion identify as appropriate and useful for encouraging play and learning.

Toys and Materials: This checklist identifies toys and materials appropriate for children in each of the three developmental periods. It is important to note that general types of toys are identified, rather than specific or brand-name toys.

Physical Attributes of the Environment: Room and furniture arrangement is a critical element in designing settings that support early development. This checklist identifies key factors to consider when designing play spaces for young children. We have also provided sample room arrangements in Appendix B.

Do's and Don'ts

The interactions of parents and other significant adults are probably the most important factor in enhancing early development. Yes, we all care about play materials and environmental setups, but the activities and behaviors of the caregiver are so important that they are given great attention in *Childmate*. In particular, we offer extra help by listing specific do's and don'ts.

Each of us has learned ways of living and being with young children. The "Do's and Don'ts" sections of *Childmate* highlight common themes and practices related to quality interactions between caregivers and children in each developmental phase. The focus of these recommended practices is important for the developing child.

Acknowledgments

We appreciate the reviewers' time and effort, and value the contributions they made to the manuscript. Thanks to:

Jennifer Aldrich, Ed.D

Central Missouri State University
Warrensburg, MO

Billie Armstrong

Tyrrell County Head Start
Columbia, NC

Jennifer Berke, Ph.D.

Mercyhurst College, North East
North East, PA

Irene Cook

California State University, Bakersfield
Bakersfield, CA

Mary Henthorne

Western Wisconsin Technical College
LaCrosse, WI

Karen Manning

Kiddie Academy
Albany, NY

Judy Rose-Paterson

Pilgrim's Children Center
Carlsbad, CA

Brenda Schin

Private Child Care Provider
Ballston Spa, NY

Sandy Wlaschin

University of Nebraska–Omaha
Omaha, NE

Introduction

Parents desire the best for their children. They want their children to be happy, healthy, and successful. Parents are their child's primary teachers; in fact, they have the greatest and longest lasting influence on their child's life. Caregivers must communicate respect for a parent's role in the child's life. As well as talking with parents about their child's favorite play routines, ways of communicating, special needs, and unique signs and signals, caregivers will want to discuss parent priorities and goals and parenting activities that reflect the family's cultural traditions. Caregivers will want to establish a variety of ways for communicating with parents. Activities such as notes, home-school journals, conversations, family meetings, workshops, parent support groups, conferences, and advisory committees are all potential activities for establishing strong partnerships with families.

- Program staff partner with each family by having conversations with the family to gather information about their child, experiences, and child-rearing beliefs.
- Program staff has daily interactions with parents to gather information from, and share information about, their child.
- Program staff provides opportunities for family members to participate in program decisions and governance, advocate for themselves, and serve as resources to other parents.

Family Culture and Traditions Are the Context of Early Development

Families come in all shapes, sizes, and traditions. A decision to work closely with children and families assumes a responsibility to recognize, understand, support, and celebrate these differences. Recognizing that cultural learning starts at birth, caregivers must themselves become familiar with each family's cultural traditions. Children learn what is expected of them and what to expect from others through the cultural messages passed on from parents, grandparents, and other significant adults. These messages shape a child's understanding of everything, from touch, positioning of one's body, what is regarded as mannerly, and how one thinks, senses time, and perceives space to beliefs about what is important and how to set immediate and lifelong goals. The ideal is for families and caregivers to be involved in a joint process that ensures that children thrive within their respective cultures. In the process, children may become bicultural. It is important, however, to assure that becoming competent in another culture adds to what a child already has and does not replace the cultural traditions of the family of origin. When children enter an environment that gives them mixed or competing messages about what is expected or acceptable, they begin to question their actions; cultural foundations that have been established no longer provide the safety and security they need to be assertive and take risks (Brand & ~~relopment~~ 999). Appendix A lists resources for exploring cultural urally sensitive practice in early childhood education.

staff is provided with opportunities to explore their own nd and beliefs about parenting and caring for young

re provided with authentic opportunities to share ion about their culture and child-rearing values. ulture is evident in the ways in which staff interacts with children and families and makes decisions about materials and activities.

Quality Care Depends on Quality Relationships

Young children need caring, nurturing, responsive environments. When children spend time in communities where they feel safe and valued, where their physical needs are met, and where they are psychologically secure, they develop a sense of security and the knowledge that they are cared for and cared about. Children who feel safe, supported, and cared about are better able to explore, experiment, and master the world. Characteristics of nurturing and responsive communities include:

- Daily routines and plans are flexible and easily adapted to the needs and interests of individual children and the group as a whole.
- Program staff listen and respond to children's needs, discoveries, interests and provide support when children are frustrated.
- Staff systematically observes each child to discover what skills the child is working on, his or her approach to learning and exploration, and his or her interaction style.

Environments Are Child Centered

Because children learn best when they are passionately involved in their own learning, caregivers can foster children's learning and development by building on their interests, needs, and strengths. In child-centered environments, children create their own knowledge from their experiences and interactions with the world around them (Hansen, Kaufman, & Walsh, 1996). Whether working with an infant who loves to listen to music, a toddler who is determined to climb, or a preschooler who has been transformed into a superhero, caregivers who set up environments that speak to a child's inner soul will encourage children's natural curiosity and foster cooperative learning. In effect, when caregivers take advantage of a child's interests and play, they begin a dance for learning. In this dance, both the caregiver and the child will take turns leading, inquiring, and responding. The message of the dance will be vibrant: go ahead, explore, initiate, and create. Ways to do this may include:

- Children are provided with uninterrupted time to explore.
- Staff has a daily plan that includes activities and materials that are appropriate for children's interests and abilities and do not require adult direction.
- Children are encouraged to use materials to express themselves.

Individualize the Learning Experience

Individualizing the learning experience reminds us that each child is unique. Young children differ in their biological rhythms, their likes and dislikes, and the ways they use their senses and skills to make sense of the world around them. Caregivers who understand each child's unique style and temperament are prepared to be responsive to individual needs and cues rather than expecting children to conform to adult routines, schedules, and expectations. Individualization requires that caregivers create activities that enable each child to be successful as well as challenged. Environments that are child centered provide a wonderful context for supporting individualized learning. For example, two children sitting at the same art center may interact with the materials in very different ways. While one may work for half an hour with scissors, glue, and markers to create a fairy house, the other may quickly make bright yellow marks and announce, "Mr. Golden Sun." Clearly, once the caregiver arranges the furniture and sets out the materials, the children are free to engage at their own levels and express their own interests in the materials.

- Staff understands and supports each child's temperamental style.
- Staff analyzes the environment to ensure materials, activities, and adult behaviors are responsive to each child's abilities and needs.

- Staff adapts its behaviors to meet the needs and interests of all children.

Children Learn Through Play

Play is at the center of good early childhood programs. Play occurs in variety of ways: solitary play with objects; unstructured, associative play with one other child; interactive and complex dramatic play with props and other children; and more structured play in group games as children get older. By definition, play is self initiated and self directed. Play is pleasurable, has no extrinsic goals (goals such as curiosity or a desire to master a skill come from within the child), is spontaneous, involves the child's active engagement, and is characterized by pretense (not constrained by reality) (Garvey, 1977, p. 4). For infants, play is best described as manipulative. Babies bang, shake, push, pull, turn, and manipulate objects to discover what they are and what they do. Toddlers and preschoolers enter the world of symbolic play, spending time in make-believe. Early symbolic play provides a context for children to replay familiar scenes such as cleaning, cooking, or going to the grocery store. Older children will often create complex play scenes involving scripts and a host of real and imagined characters. Play forms the foundation for the development of intellect, creativity, and a sense of self. Through their play, children express their feelings and develop the capacity to form relationships with others.

- Play materials are organized so that they are easily accessible and children can use them appropriately.
- Children are provided with uninterrupted time to explore and create.
- Adults support children's explorations, converse with children about their discoveries, and support their testing of how things work.

The challenge of providing quality care for children is immense. We have learned that excellent early childhood programs are created when caregivers continually analyze and adjust the environment to engage, challenge, and support the young child's learning. In short, quality programs result from intentional planning (Hull, Goldhaber, & Capone, 2002).

Online Resources™

The Online Resources™ to accompany *Childmate: A Guide to Appraising Quality in Child Care* is your link to early childhood education on the Internet. The Online Resources™ contain many features to help focus your understanding of quality child care:

- Contact Information—you will be able to conduct further research on quality child care with contact information for federal and state organizations and licensing departments.
- Forms—you will find downloadable/printable versions of the checklists found throughout *Childmate: A Guide to Appraising Quality in Child Care.*
- Do's and Don'ts—you will find downloadable/printable versions of the lists of Do's and Don'ts, which you can print easily for reference.

 The Online Resources™ icon appears at the end of each chapter to prompt you to go on-line and take advantage of the many features provided.

You can find the Online Resources™ at www.earlychilded.delmar.com

Infancy
(2 to 12 Months)

Eight-month-old Caleigh sits in her carriage, bright-eyed, smiling, and full of excitement. The neighborhood children are out playing ball and she wants to be part of the action. Her laughter and reaching hands help her accomplish her goal. Within seconds Caleigh has captured a bright green ball and finds herself surrounded by six adoring toddlers and preschoolers who imitate and laugh at her smiles and sounds.

Developmental Overview of Infancy (2 to 12 Months)

Anyone who has spent time with infants would easily agree that the first year of life is one of tremendous growth and development. Infancy is a time of active and continuous learning, in which children acquire skills that form the basis for dealing with their surroundings and connecting with people. Over the course of the first twelve months, infants develop attachments to significant adults in their lives; become mobile; coordinate their actions to solve simple problems, comprehend words, and use gestures meaningfully; and communicate with the world around them.

Human Connectedness

Human connectedness, or attachment, is one of the most significant accomplishments of the first year. The attachment process involves establishing close relationships between an infant and significant people in the child's world (Ainsworth, 1974; Sroufe & Waters, 1977). Although attachment with early childhood caregivers differs from an

infant's attachment with parents, it is no less important. Recent research suggests that the attachment an infant forms with primary early childhood caregivers provides a secure or trusting base from which to explore and participate in the environment. Attachment to an early childhood caregiver enhances communication and assures that the infant's needs are understood and attended to. Through attachment, children know that they are cared about, as well as cared for (Gonzales-Mena & Eyer, 1997).

Although it may seem incredible, from the moment of birth, infants are competent partners in shaping early relationships. Infants enter the world well suited to engage with caregivers in a "dance of interaction and attachment" (Stern, 1977). Infants are primed to interact with caregivers. During feeding, the adult's face is at an optimum distance from the baby's eyes. The human face, particularly the eyes and mouth, are just the sort of visual stimuli at which an infant is most likely to look. Faces are an infant's favorite and most important toys. Infants are also particularly sensitive to the human voice.

Adult behaviors are critical during the first six months, when infants are sharply focused on the people in their environments. Caregivers must be prepared to respond to infants in a manner that encourages attachment (Greenman, 1988). The ordinary exchanges that occur between infant and caregiver (such as looking, gazing, cooing, verbal and tactile play, and smiling) are critical experiences through which the infant learns how to relate to others. It is important that these exchanges be respectful, responsive, and reciprocal (Gonzales-Mena & Eyer, 1997).

Exploratory Play

By about six months, the infant's infatuation with the human face, voice, and touch expands to include an intense interest in objects. The maturation that has occurred in the infant's motor, visual, and cognitive systems drives interest in reaching for, grasping, and manipulating objects. This early exploratory play is serious business. Not only does exploration play a critical role in the development of sensorimotor intelligence, but there is also a strong, positive relationship between the amount of exploratory play and the confidence and ease with which the child approaches new situations and materials. A tremendous amount of shaking, banging, and mouthing of objects characterizes exploratory play. These efforts yield information about the objects in the surrounding world.

Through touching [the infant] learns [the objects'] shapes, dimensions, slopes, edges, and textures. He also fingers, grasps, pushes, and pulls and thus learns the material variables of heaviness, mass, and rigidity, as well as the changes in visual and auditory stimuli that objects provide. . . . In a word, he learns the properties of the physical world, including the principles of object constancy and the conservation of matter. (Rheingold & Eckerman, 1971, p. 78)

The emergence of exploratory play has a dramatic impact on the relationship between the infant and caregiver. While the caregiver remains essential, the play becomes a "triadic affair" among the infant, caregiver, and object (Stern, 1977). The caregiver now assumes more of supporting role in the object-play sessions that will be the focus of many of the infant's awake hours. The exploration that begins in infancy will continue to dominate the infant's time now and throughout the early years.

Clearly, the first year of life is a busy and event-filled time for infants, parents, and caregivers. By the end of the first year, the infant's social capabilities are formidable. Through exploratory play, the infant has begun to develop an understanding of the objects and events that comprise the surrounding world. These tremendous accomplishments occur within environments that are sensitive and responsive to the infant's growing competence. The infant's unique dependence on adults challenges caregivers to respond in a manner that facilitates the development of attachment, relationships, and exploratory play behaviors. Caregivers are also constantly challenged to evaluate and change their behaviors in response to the infant's evolving perceptual and physical abilities.

Guiding Principles for Supporting Optimal Development in Group Care Settings

Make Movement Activities a High Priority

In the words of an old adage, "Babies learn to move and babies learn through movement." Movement is an incredibly important activity throughout infancy. Through their actions and the environment's response to those actions, infants develop a basic understanding of cause-effect relationships; the use of objects as tools; and sequence, classification, and spatial relationships. As infants explore objects and people, they become aware of how their bodies move and feel. Through the repetition of actions, infants develop motor skills and physical strength. Infants who have numerous and varied opportunities for movement and exploration soon discover they can change what they see, hear, and feel through their own activity.

Make Multisensory Experience Available

There is a strong link between motor and sensory experiences. Infants are constantly involved in the process of gathering and processing the information they receive through their senses. When we say that infants learn through sensing, we are referring to the vast amount of information they receive through the five senses: hearing, smell, taste, touch, and sight. It is important that infants receive input to each sense and that they be allowed to explore the world through their senses.

Treat the Infant As Your Partner

Infants should be considered partners in everything that involves them. Whether changing a diaper, warming food for lunch, or playing with a toy, caregivers should engage in a conversation with the infant about the event. The depth of attention infants demonstrate when they are engaged is amazing to observe. By recognizing and supporting infants as active participants, we provide opportunities for them to discover that they can influence the people and things that surround them. Each experience provides that infant with an essential opportunity to master the environment, grow cognitively, and become more purposeful. Caregivers should be careful not to rush an infant who is exploring an object or event or to overwhelm an infant with quick movements, fast speech, or too much physical clutter.

Keep Alert for Infant Discomfort and Need for Help

Babies have not yet developed the ability to cope with discomfort. Caregivers must become adept at recognizing and responding to the many ways an infant has of saying, "I'm not happy, please help me," or, "I'm really interested in this, please talk to me about it." Infants may tell you they are feeling stress or discomfort by doing the following:

- hiccuping, gagging, sighing, coughing, sneezing, or yawning
- spreading fingers apart (splaying their hands)
- saluting
- frowning, grimacing, or grunting
- arching their back and pushing away
- crying, looking away
- clenching their fists

As a caring adult, you can respond to an infant's statement of stress or discomfort by doing the following:

- laying the infant quietly on your lap
- talking to the infant softly
- providing quiet time
- interacting slowly and using a calm face, soft voice, and gentle touch
- wrapping the infant in a blanket
- putting the infant down in a safe, quiet place

Checklists

Caregiver Behaviors

The behaviors of caregivers are key to quality experiences for young children. Observation, reflection, adaptation, and planning are key characteristics for responsive caregiving.

Check the appropriate box.

Make Movement Activities a High Priority. Infants learn through action. Through their actions and the environment's response to those actions, infants develop a basic understanding of cause and effect, sequencing, classification, objects as tools, and spatial relationships.

Caregiver	Not Yet	Occasionally	Frequently	Typically
1. Plays simple movement/singing games with infant.	☐	☐	☐	☐
2. Provides opportunities for infants to reach for, pull, and grasp playthings.	☐	☐	☐	☐
3. Provides opportunities for infant to develop balance and movement skills.	☐	☐	☐	☐
4. Fosters independence by encouraging infant to pull off socks, use a cup, use a spoon, etc.	☐	☐	☐	☐
5. Provides opportunities for infant to find objects that are hidden under blankets, bowls, etc.	☐	☐	☐	☐
6. Encourages the infant to stack, unwrap, and transfer objects in and out of containers.	☐	☐	☐	☐
7. Provides activities that allow the infant to throw/drop objects.	☐	☐	☐	☐

continued

Caregiver	Not Yet	Occasionally	Frequently	Typically
8. Provides opportunities for infant to play with objects that are related to one another such as: dump truck and sand, comb and brush, spoon and bowl.	☐	☐	☐	☐

Comments:

_____

_____

_____

Make Multisensory Experience Available. Infants are sensuous beings. It is important that infants receive input to each sense and that they be allowed to explore the world through their senses.

Caregiver	Not Yet	Occasionally	Frequently	Typically
9. Provides the infant opportunities to explore different textures such as smooth, rough, slippery.	☐	☐	☐	☐
10. Places infant in different positions and locations in the room for play.	☐	☐	☐	☐
11. Provides a variety of sounds for infant to listen to.	☐	☐	☐	☐
12. Places infant in front of mirrors with toys to enable the infant to watch own play.	☐	☐	☐	☐
13. Provides the infant the experience of moving through space.	☐	☐	☐	☐
14. Offers opportunities for infant to act on the environment to learn cause and effect, e.g., open doors, remove covers, push buttons and switches, etc.	☐	☐	☐	☐
15. Provides objects that make sounds in response to a variety of actions by the infant.	☐	☐	☐	☐

Caregiver	Not Yet	Occasionally	Frequently	Typically
16. Provides an environment that is visually appealing and stimulating, including objects that are brightly colored and those that make noise as they are moved.	☐	☐	☐	☐

Comments:

_____

_____

_____

Treat the Infant as Your Partner. Infants are active participants in their environment and should be considered partners in everything that involves them. Each experience provides the infant with an essential opportunity to master the environment, grow cognitively, and become more purposeful.

Caregiver	Not Yet	Occasionally	Frequently	Typically
17. Imitates infant's sounds while adding inflections; encourages the infant to repeat the sound.	☐	☐	☐	☐
18. Tells the infant what is about to happen.	☐	☐	☐	☐
19. Describes what is occurring during routines (diapering, bathing, feeding).	☐	☐	☐	☐
20. Talks about what the infant is exploring without being distracting.	☐	☐	☐	☐
21. Includes the infant in conversation and identifies the people and actions that are taking place.	☐	☐	☐	☐
22. Encourages language development by asking questions or interpreting the infant's behavior.	☐	☐	☐	☐
23. Encourages the infant to imitate simple actions (e.g., touch nose, look up, hold arms out).	☐	☐	☐	☐

continued

Caregiver	Not Yet	Occasionally	Frequently	Typically
24. Shows glee (smiles, hugs, comments) when an infant attempts new skills or shows improvement.	☐	☐	☐	☐
25. Reads, sings, and repeats rhymes with infants.	☐	☐	☐	☐

Comments:

_____

_____

_____

Keep Alert for Infant Discomfort and Need for Help. **Infants are vulnerable and have not yet developed the ability to cope with discomfort. Early educators must become adept at recognizing and responding to infant cues.**

Caregiver	Not Yet	Occasionally	Frequently	Typically
26. Immediately detects and reacts to infant signals of possible risk (e.g., eye contact, widening eyes, waving arms, reaching, back arching).	☐	☐	☐	☐
27. Can tell the difference between types of cries (e.g., tired, hungry, in discomfort, frightened).	☐	☐	☐	☐

Comments:

_____

_____

_____

Toys and Materials

Toys and other play materials are the tools that help infants begin constructing their understanding of the world. Carefully chosen objects will encourage the development of concepts such as cause and effect, spatial relationships, and classification. In addition, objects will spark curiosity and excitement and encourage the infant to explore the world. It is important to note, however, that people and faces are the most important objects in an infant's world. Toys and other play materials should not replace the infant's interactions with adults and each other.

	NO	YES
There are interesting objects for infants to look at such as:		
1. Hanging objects with interesting shapes, textures, and sounds	☐	☐
2. Bright scarves	☐	☐
3. Unbreakable mirrors	☐	☐
4. Photos of family members	☐	☐
There are a variety of objects to touch and manipulate such as these:		
5. Rattles of different sizes, shapes, and textures	☐	☐
6. Soft toys (e.g., soft balls, stuffed animals, squeeze toys)	☐	☐
7. Containers for dumping and filling	☐	☐
8. Peg toys that bring together elements of sorting and concepts of in and out	☐	☐
9. Play materials that are responsive to child's action	☐	☐
10. Large plastic beads	☐	☐
11. Plastic keys	☐	☐
12. Softballs of different sizes and textures	☐	☐
13. Roly-poly toys with weighted bottoms	☐	☐
14. Boxes of all sizes with lids	☐	☐

continued

	NO	YES
15. Blocks: lightweight for throwing and stacking, heavy blocks for grasp and release	☐	☐
16. Everyday objects that are safe: pots, pans, wooden spoons, unbreakable cups, containers	☐	☐
17. Nesting toys: for handling and manipulation	☐	☐
There are materials that encourage sensory exploration such as:		
18. Carpet squares of various textures for tactile experiences	☐	☐
19. Squeeze/squeaky toys	☐	☐
20. Materials for tactile experiences (e.g., liquids, solids such as cornmeal)	☐	☐
21. Variety of paper to tear	☐	☐
22. Water toys to allow infants to explore concepts of movement and motion	☐	☐
23. Bells	☐	☐
There are toys that encourage movement such as:		
24. Pull toys	☐	☐
25. Plastic or wooden cars and trucks	☐	☐
26. Equipment to climb on, crawl into, pull upon, hold onto		
There are materials that foster early literacy such as:		
27. Picture books	☐	☐
28. Board books	☐	☐
29. Photo albums	☐	☐

Comments:

_____

_____

_____

Physical Attributes of the Environment

The physical environment is yet another critical variable for quality early care and education programs. The physical environment can promote or impede the development of satisfying relationships, child-to-child interactions, and exploration and play. In addition, the physical environment should feel welcoming and supportive for family members. As with all sections of *Childmate,* this section does not stand alone. As you reflect on this checklist, consider how the components relate to your space, the children who attend your program and your curricula goals. Your challenge will be to integrate this information with your own experience and knowledge as well as the information presented in other sections of *Childmate.* Remember the goal, as always, is to create an environment that motivates children to interact, explore, grow, and learn. See Appendix B for sample room arrangements and arrangement rationales.

	NO	YES
The facility has equipment and features such as:		
1. Cribs that allow infant to look out and around	☐	☐
2. Wall decorations that provide color and interesting pictures to look at	☐	☐
3. Pictures that are at the infant's eye level	☐	☐
4. A variety of sounds and music	☐	☐
5. Rocking chairs for adults to rock babies	☐	☐
6. An area of the room that is quiet and calming	☐	☐
7. A space for infants to be protected from older and/or mobile children	☐	☐
8. Rails or small, sturdy furniture that help the infant stand or cruise about	☐	☐
9. An open area in the center of the room that may be used as a hub for activities	☐	☐
10. Accessible storage areas (yet out of the reach of children) for items that are used on a consistent or emergency basis	☐	☐
11. An area of the room where the floor is carpeted or matted	☐	☐

continued

	NO	YES
12. A sleeping area that is separated from the play area	☐	☐
13. Soft colors in curtains, pillows, and sheets	☐	☐
14. Bright accent pieces	☐	☐
15. Music available for soothing, dancing, and singing	☐	☐
16. Cubbies for each child	☐	☐
17. Space for communicating with parents about daily events; feeding, changing, and sleeping schedules	☐	☐
18. Storage cupboards for extra materials or materials that are used inconsistently	☐	☐
19. Outdoor play area with protection from the sun	☐	☐
20. An acoustically calm environment	☐	☐
21. Natural soft lighting (limit or eliminate the use of fluorescent lights)	☐	☐
22. Shelves for displaying toys at child level (shelves should be anchored to the wall)	☐	☐
23. Furniture positioned so that infants can explore each other	☐	☐
24. A space for breast-feeding	☐	☐
25. Clear pathways for infants and adults to move about the space	☐	☐
26. Space for having private conversations with parents	☐	☐
27. Space for parents to visit with each other	☐	☐

Comments:

_____

_____

_____

Do's and Don'ts

To provide quality experiences for young children, you can do the following:

1. ## Play simple movement/singing games with infant.

    DO

    - ☑ Play Peek-a-Boo; This Little Piggy Went to Market; Wheels on the Bus; Pat-a-Cake; Row, Row, Row Your Boat.
    - ☑ Bounce infant on knee to simple songs or play "This is the Way the Ladies Ride."
    - ☑ Dance with the infant.
    - ☑ Provide music of all types.

    DON'T Provide music only to distract or put infant to sleep.

2. ## Provide opportunity for infant to reach for, pull, and grasp playthings.

    DO

    - ☑ Make objects available to the infant such as small squeeze toys, teething rings, and rattles.
    - ☑ Encourage younger infant to reach for object such as dangling toys in a crib.
    - ☑ Encourage the child to reach repeatedly for objects that were not accessible initially (favorite toy).
    - ☑ Give the object to the child after a few attempts if the infant is unable to get it.
    - ☑ Place toys in different locations (on a low shelf, in a box) and encourage the infant to get them.

☑ Place objects in such a way that infant must turn or twist to retrieve them.

DON'T Just give objects to the infant, but also do not place them in locations where they are impossible for the infant to retrieve.

3. **Provide opportunities for infant to develop balance and movement skills.**

   DO

   ☑ Encourage younger infant to practice protective reflexes (e.g., hold infant at waist and gently let him or her fall forward).

   ☑ Encourage infant to roll, creep, or crawl to favorite toys.

   ☑ Encourage infant to go up and down equipment with small steps.

   ☑ Allow infant to pull to stand and provide opportunities to cruise while holding onto furniture, etc.

   DON'T Keep infant in cribs or playpens; have dirty, hard, or cold floors that discourage movements; or allow an environment that is crowded or unsafe.

4. **Foster independence by encouraging the infant to pull off socks or use a cup or spoon.**

   DO

   ☑ Encourage the infant to pull off socks.

   ☑ Encourage the infant to use a cup, spoon, etc.

   DON'T Do things for an infant that he/she can do independently.

5. Provide opportunities for the infant to find objects that are hidden under blankets, bowls, etc.

DO

☑ Play Peek-a-Boo.

☑ Place infant next to caregiver with a favorite toy hidden behind the caregiver's back, in a box, or behind a barrier. Encourage infant to look for or reach for the toy.

☑ Place objects under cloths or containers and encourage the infant to find them.

☑ Move toys behind a screen or barrier and bring them out on the other side, encouraging the infant to anticipate the reappearance.

☑ Encourage the infant to look for objects that have been dropped or have disappeared from the infant's sight (use objects that make a sound when hitting the floor).

DON'T Tease the infant by moving objects around from under screens or barriers where they were first placed.

6. Encourage infants to stack, unwrap, and transfer objects in and out of containers.

DO

☑ Offer opportunities to nest differently shaped boxes and cans. Provide assistance when needed.

☑ Provide boxes, blocks, or cans for stacking. Demonstrate stacking and knocking them down. Encourage infant to gather fallen objects.

☑ Wrap a favorite toy in waxed paper or newspaper as the infant watches and encourage him or her to unwrap it.

☑ Provide rings for infant to stack and take off.

☑ Provide large foam boards or other cylindrical objects that can be fitted in a hole.

☑ Provide infant with insertion toys (large pegboard, large beads).

DON'T Restrict the kinds of toys and activities.

7. Provide activities that allow the infant to throw and drop objects.

DO

☑ Provide infant with beanbags and balls of various sizes and textures to throw.

☑ Provide opportunities for infant to throw blocks into container or crumpled paper into a wastebasket.

☑ Encourage infant to drop balls, beanbags, or other objects into a container.

DON'T Show approval when the infant drops or throws objects inappropriately. (Don't make a "pick-up game" out of the behavior.)

DON'T Restrict opportunities for infant to throw or drop objects or fail to provide appropriate materials for this activity.

8. Provide opportunities for infants to play with objects that are related to one another such as brush/comb, dump truck/sand, spoon/bowl.

DO

☑ Play games by taking one of the objects and asking the infant for the object it goes with.

☑ Allow 10 to 15 seconds for the baby to find or ask for the matching object.

DON'T Wait too long to show the matching object.

9. **Provide infants with opportunities to explore different textures.**

   DO

   ☑ Use a variety of textures such as silk, velvet, corduroy, fur, flannel, and cottons.

   ☑ Use toys that have different textures such as soft, smooth, bumpy, rough, or hard or that vibrate.

   ☑ Tell the infant what parts of his or her body are being rubbed.

   ☑ Provide an older infant (4–6 months) with large household items such as unused scrub brushes.

   ☑ Inspect items to be sure they can not be taken apart or swallowed.

   ☑ Place infant on different textures (grass mat, blanket, hardwood floor) and encourage him or her to explore textures.

   ☑ Describe properties of foods the infant is eating ("The banana is soft and mushy.")

   DON'T Continue to give baby textures that he or she does not like or only one or two different textures.

10. **Place infant in different positions and different locations in the room for play.**

    DO

    ☑ Hold infant in different positions while walking with him or her: over different shoulders, facing toward then away, etc.

    ☑ Place infant on the back, side, or stomach while playing with a toy.

    ☑ Allow infant to see different perspectives of the environment by swinging, sitting in a stroller, sitting on the floor, or lying on the floor in different positions.

    ☑ Place infant in different parts of the room.

    DON'T Keep infant in a crib or playpen too long.

11. Provide opportunities for infants to listen to a variety of sounds.

DO

- ☑ Put infant in a position to search for sounds visually.
- ☑ Identify sounds as they occur.
- ☑ Provide a variety of music for infant.
- ☑ Make available a variety of sounds such as the sound of a clock, dial tone, noisemakers, squeaky toys, crumpled paper, click of a light switch, running water, musical instruments.

DON'T Overwhelm the infant with too much stimulation!

12. Place the infant in front of mirrors with toys to watch his or her play.

DO

- ☑ Show infant simple games to play in front of the mirror (Pat-a-Cake, body part naming songs).
- ☑ Encourage infant to notice his or her reflection in the mirror.
- ☑ Encourage infant to touch reflections of him- or herself, toys, or colorful puppets.

DON'T Have baby too far from mirror (about 2 feet is best).

13. Provide opportunities for the infant to experience moving through space.

DO

- ☑ Play piggy-back, give wagon rides, and swing infant.

DON'T Move too quickly or abruptly or otherwise frighten the infant.

14. **Offer the infant a variety of opportunities to see how actions involve cause and effect.**

    DO

    ☑ Provide a variety of toys that can manually be put into action: windup cars/trucks, friction cars/trucks, toys that have parts that move when pushed or pulled, toys that make sounds when used.

    ☑ Explain the action that is occurring.

    ☑ Repeat a cause-effect action so that it can be anticipated.

    ☑ Allow child to explore object properties.

    ☑ Provide objects that work together or have a novel effect on child's environment (stick/drum, wooden hammer and pounding bench, spoons and things to stir, shovel and pail).

    DON'T Simply explain cause-effect; let infant actually see, hear, or feel an effect.

15. **Provide infant with objects that make sounds in response to a variety of the infant's actions.**

    DO

    ☑ Offer infant toys that squeak or rattle.

    ☑ Allow infant to hit or bang appropriate toys to make sound (musical instruments, cans).

    ☑ Provide toys that produce sound when pushed or pulled.

    DON'T Discourage infant from banging or hitting appropriate objects to make sounds.

16. Provide an environment that is visually appealing and stimulating, including objects that are brightly colored and those that make noise as they are moved.

DO

☑ Place objects from home in obvious places in the room.

☑ Show the baby pictures of a face, geometric forms, a mirror, a shiny pinwheel, colorful scarves, balloons, etc.

☑ Move objects slowly across infant's view.

☑ Present objects that baby can see and hear such as brightly colored rattles and musical toys.

DON'T Show items to baby too quickly or abruptly.

17. Imitate infant's sounds, add inflections, and encourage the infant to repeat the sound.

DO

☑ React promptly to the infant's sounds.

☑ "Make faces" and gestures/encourage eye contact.

☑ Use a variety of intonations or inflections such as "happy."

☑ Show enjoyment while imitating infant's sounds.

☑ Reproduce sounds an infant makes and encourage the infant to imitate them.

☑ Repeat mouth actions such as lip popping.

☑ Exaggerate facial and mouth movements to keep infant's attention. Play "I'm Going to Get You" or tickle the infant.

☑ Make animal sounds like those of a dog, cat, cow, or horse.

☑ Sing simple nursery rhymes and songs that contain simple movements that are related to specific words.

☑ Take time to talk to infant in a pleasant voice and allow time for the infant to respond.

DON'T Interrupt an infant who is making happy, babbling sounds or use a loud voice that might frighten the baby.

18. Tell infant what is about to happen.

DO

☑ Call infant's name while approaching.

☑ Talk to the infant before he or she can see you.

☑ Tell infant what is about to happen, using phrases such as, "I'm going to pick you up," or "Let's go look out the window."

☑ Tell older infant what is about to occur during transition periods (from playing to feeding, from feeding to bathing).

DON'T Move infant from one activity or location to another without saying or signaling what is going to happen next.

19. Describe what is occurring during routines (diapering, bathing, feeding).

DO

☑ Explain to infant in playful ways what is going on during routine events.

DON'T Remain silent during activities or act harshly or roughly (verbally or physically) during routines.

20. **Talk about what the child is exploring without being distracting.**

   DO

   ☑ Offer comments and encouragement about what the infant is doing while not interrupting the play.

   DON'T Distract infant from play by unnecessary interruptions or suddenly introducing a new activity.

21. **Include infant in conversation and identify people and actions that are taking place.**

   DO

   ☑ Identify people and repeat names of objects in the infant's surroundings (Mamma, Daddy, diaper, bottle, rattle, window, tree, etc.).

   ☑ Examine a new toy with the infant and talk about the toy as the infant plays with it.

   ☑ Describe to infant what is about to occur, what is occurring, and what has already happened. "We're going to have lunch. First, let's change your diaper. There, your diaper is changed."

   ☑ Talk with, sing, and read to infant.

   DON'T Use limited vocabulary or move infant around without explanation.

22. **Encourage language development by asking questions or interpreting the infant's behavior.**

   DO

   ☑ Ask infant to locate objects around the room ("Where is the _____?")

   ☑ Narrate what the infant is doing with phrases such as, "Look at you, banging that block."

☑ Use action words in giving simple commands such as: shake, wave, give. ("Shake the rattle." "Give me your shoe." "Wave bye-bye to Daddy.")

☑ Place familiar objects (ball, shoe, block, etc.) in front of infant and ask, "Find me the _____." or "Where is the _____?"

☑ Emphasize appropriate inflection when asking questions or giving simple commands.

DON'T Avoid opportunities for infant to show understanding.

23. ## Encourage infant to imitate actions of caregiver (e.g., touch nose, look up, hold arms out).

DO

☑ Imitate actions of the infant during play.

☑ Play singing games with the infant that involve imitative play (Pat-a-Cake; The Wheels on the Bus; If You're Happy and You Know It, Clap Your Hands; Peek-a-Boo).

DON'T Remove items from infant that are being used in imitative play because the materials are messy.

24. ## Show glee (smiles, hugs, comments) when an infant attempts a new skill or shows improvement.

DO

☑ Select play materials based on each child's interests.

☑ Share emerging interests and skills with parents.

☑ Use voice inflections and facial expressions that communicate delight.

☑ Change the environment to reflect new skills and interests.

DON'T Restrict children from using new skills or pursuing new interests through lack of reinforcement or limiting opportunities.

25. Read, sing, and repeat rhymes with infants.

DO

☑ Have a variety of books, photo albums, pictures to look at and talk about.

☑ Use nursery rhymes and short, repetitive songs and rhyming language.

DON'T Use books with too many words rather than pictures.

26. Immediately detect and react to the infant's signals (e.g., eye contact, widening eyes, waving arms, and reaching) of possible risk.

DO

☑ Smile, touch, talk to or pick up a child to initiate social interaction.

DON'T Ignore infant's attempts to interact or do things that are unpredictable or that may frighten infant.

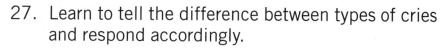

27. Learn to tell the difference between types of cries and respond accordingly.

DO

☑ Learn to recognize meaning of an infant's different cries, such as tired, hungry, in discomfort, frightened.

☑ Know how to provide comfort for the infant.

DON'T Ignore an infant's attempt to communicate by crying.

For additional information on appraising quality child care, visit our Web site at http://www.earlychilded.delmar.com

Toddlerhood
(12 to 36 Months)

Twenty-six-month-old John arrived at child care holding tightly to Mom's hand. He had only been in this caregiving situation for three weeks, so entering was still a little difficult. Once in, he greeted his caregiver with a loud, joyful, "Teesa!" After a big hug, John noticed "Obby" (Robby, age 32 months), a favorite playmate. "Play 'ouse'," John announced. He and his friend went up to the kitchen table and began interacting with a dollhouse and set of figurines. While Robby created a scenario of "Mommy get up," "Daddy go to work," and "Silas eat breakfast," John put "Mommy" in and out of doors and windows. Each time John's "Mommy figure" went in the house, John would say "Mommy in." Each time Mommy went out a window or door, John would say, "Mommy out." This parallel play scene lasted for ten minutes. The play ended as both boys jumped down to join other children racing cars across the playroom floor.

Developmental Overview of Toddlerhood (12 to 36 Months)

We all agree that infants are a marvel; their incredible physical growth and development of skills seem almost magical. But *toddlers* are the great entertainers. Being around a group of toddlers is like being surrounded by comedians who continually do and say the funniest things. This is a time when children are in "high gear" as they play, race about, question everything, experiment with emerging skills, and get into everything! Toddlerhood is a time when temperamental characteristics become clear, social growth is in full swing, and play becomes the center of life. The toddler increasingly tells you, "I do it myself." There is also a clear and strong kind of demanding at this time: the "toddler tyrant" appears to issue demands and is upset if not satisfied. What a time of life! Certainly, quality care and parenting are essential, and the stress on parents and caregivers, not to mention the children, can be considerable if care is haphazard or punitive. Toddlerhood, ages 1 to 3, must be cherished: it is all too brief.

Autonomy (I'll Do It Myself!)

As children grow and develop through the toddler years, autonomy, or "executive independence" (Ausubel, 1959), becomes a dominant theme and accomplishment. Toddlers strive for increasing control over their environments. As they mature and learn to walk and manipulate things, they become more and more capable of doing things on their own. Yet think of the frustrations encountered: objects too high to reach, doors that cannot be opened, lids that cannot be removed, and wants that cannot be expressed. It is no wonder that toddler time is also tantrum time! But although there are continued frustrations, toddlers also begin to experience more and more success in getting around, operating on their surroundings, and getting their way. Not only do physical skills such as walking and manipulating build autonomy, but early language skills enable toddlers to begin to better express their needs and wants. Additionally, toddlers become great imitators. The "monkey see, monkey do" capability further enables toddlers to learn how to do things. Toddlers will try to mimic their older siblings; they will go through the

same motions, even if they do not accomplish the same tasks. Consider the toddler who turns through the pages of a book, pretending to read.

This is a time when children begin to group items, sorting and categorizing. Toddlers become almost compulsive about having a place for everything and everything in its place. They insist that they can do things the way they want to, and they want to do things the way they can. Defiant, possessive, and bossy qualities and increasing competence are all part of the toddler's major mission and accomplishment toward becoming a separate, independent, autonomous person.

Communication/Language Development (Let's Talk)

The acquisition and use of language are a monumental accomplishment of childhood. The toddler years are the major years when receptive and expressive language skills are rapidly established. The use of spoken language is, indeed, a major accomplishment of the human species; it is a capability that has allowed humans to achieve their dominant place on earth. So, too, the toddler's emerging language skills provide the critical tool to make possible the development of cognitive and social skills at incredible speed. The toddler initially uses much jargon, employing personal "words" to signify special objects or activities. What toddler does not have a special term for *pacifier* or *blanket*?

Toddler jargon is often put together to sound like sentences. Jargon gives way to recognized words, which are initially used to get or refer to things. Spoken vocabulary (12–24 months) can be anywhere between 5 and 50 words. Intelligibility of speech is fairly low, typically under 50 percent; of course, moms and dads can understand every word. Rhythms, rhymes, songs, and word play become major fun and learning activities. This is a time when primitive dialog appears as the toddler takes turns in a "conversation." Language development leaps forward as the toddler approaches 36 months. By this time, the toddler often uses hundreds of words, showing a continuous, remarkable explosion of word acquisition. Words are put together, with 3–4-word statements typically used. The word *no* is heard all too often but should be expected as a natural part of this developmental period (recall the defiance related to autonomy). Anyone who has spent time with a toddler knows that this is a time of endless questions: what's this, why, why not, what's that?

By the close of toddlerhood, speech is fairly intelligible (about 70 percent), but stammering and some stuttering are not uncommon. Most toddlers learn to use *I* or *me* to refer to the self, rather than own name (*I (or me) want drink* rather than *Billy want drink*). The use of pronouns signals an important landmark in development. From the infant's babbling to the toddler's jargon and, then, recognizable and fluent speech, language development is, indeed, an accomplishment of the highest priority.

Social Development (Let's Be Friends)

As important as any accomplishment, toddlers achieve the critical capacity to care about others. Empathy—sensing how others feel—is a critical attribute for developing personal relationships and becoming a

responsible, sensitive human being. (Absence of empathy is noted as a major marker of several developmental disorders, such as autism and various forms of sociopathy.) Toddlers will comfort peers and adults who appear to be in pain or sorrow. Helping to do what adults do is a delightful toddler attribute, and they will join in to do the dishes, vacuum, or feed a doll as expressions of cooperation and caring. Although able to show compassion, the toddler is still someone who can readily throw a tantrum when irritated.

Toddlers live to play and spend much of their days in either solitary or parallel play. They imitate the play of older children, but typically do not actively interact (more cooperative play comes later in the preschool years). But the skills and observations accumulated through parallel play provide the foundation for cooperative play and for the social being that the toddler will become.

Toddlerhood

Guiding Principles for Supporting Optimal Development In Group Care Settings

Arrange Safe and Engaging Situations

This is a time when physical activities are accelerating, and they will be in high gear by 24–36 months. Walking with support, "toddling," and then walking to everything becomes the major way to explore.

While infants require a rich array of stimuli to feed their senses, toddlers need numerous opportunities to play with toys and other objects that respond to their actions. Banging a drum, turning the handle on a Jack-in-the-Box, or knocking over blocks all help toddlers develop an understanding of their ability to have an effect on the world around them. Toddlers need materials, circumstances, and encouragement to do things so they will consolidate cause and effect and means-end skills.

Be sure to provide toys and materials to nurture emerging skills. Simple musical instruments (drums, xylophones, horns), safe scissors, and construction blocks are familiar examples. New battery-operated gadgets are increasingly available that provide buzzer or musical feedback when toddlers stomp on a pad or push a button. Provide foam

pads or cushions so the toddler can bounce, jump, roll, and otherwise practice physical skills. Simple games become great teaching materials as the toddler approaches preschool age. Numerous simple card games and board games teach many cognitive and social skills, such as taking turns, waiting, following rules, and remembering. Remember, the toddler wants to *play*! Therefore, the mission is to encourage learning through play, and not to force learning under the pretense of play. Remember, too, to provide choices between activities and materials. Toddlers want to make, and benefit from making, choices, another aspect of the toddler's declaration of independence.

Typically, toddlers will not initially play *with* a peer, but will play alongside a peer (parallel play). The proximity of peers while having fun, however, will result in toddlers who want to be with each other. So be sure to put two or more toddlers near each other while they are enjoying play, eating, or watching cartoons. Child care programs offer a major way to enhance socialization. Bringing up a toddler at home without playmates may not contribute to social development as well as enrolling the child in a quality child care program.

Make Communication a Two-Way Affair

The infant experiments with sounds and moves from babbling to special sounds that have special meaning: da-da, ma-ma, ba-ba. Toddlers begin to use words to express their needs, identify objects, and answer simple questions. *Receptive language* (knowing what you mean) develops rapidly. A toddler knows when someone calls his or her name. By 15 months, toddlers may point to their ear, nose, and toes when asked.

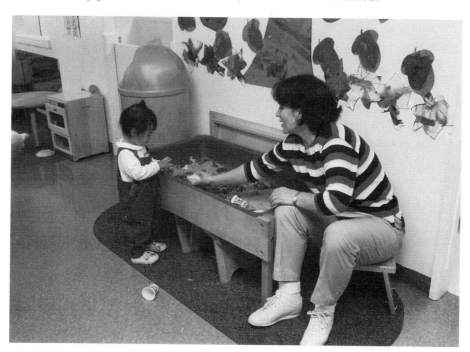

Following the growth of receptive language, expressive language also leaps ahead. The toddler calls out, continually trying to tell you what he or she wants and to name things in the environment. Talk to and with the toddler. Name things as you point or bring them to the toddler. Frequently saying the names of objects and people will help the toddler to learn the correct words for things.

Books should be a major resource. Toddlers love looking at picture books in which a few words are paired with the pictures. Looking at books together promotes cognitive and social skills as well as language development. *Reading* together can strengthen the bond between parent or caregiver and child and become a wondrous tool for learning. Because of their importance, be sure to provide quality books.

Keep the Toddler's World Organized and Routine

With all that is going on through the toddler years, making events predictable becomes truly important. Likewise, there should be a place for everything, and everything should go in its place. Toddlers love to get things and put them back where they belong. (If only we all were so organized.) Most child care programs value organization and routines, and the toddler is a natural partner in these efforts. Often, set signals (bells, music) can be used to begin or end activities. Words, pictures, or photos can be used to alert toddlers to what will happen next to reduce confusion during transitions between events.

Checklists

Caregiver Behaviors

The behaviors of caregivers are key to quality experiences for young children. Caregivers who participate in a cycle of inquiry that includes observation, reflection, and the creation of responsive learning opportunities create settings that support young children to become alert, thoughtful, and confident youngsters who, themselves, create interesting ideas, problems, and questions. Observation, reflection, adaptation, and planning are essential tools for responding to, and promoting, a young child's curiosity; in fact, they are the keys to responsive caregiving.

The following caregiver behaviors have been shown to be effective strategies for accomplishing these goals. Check the appropriate box.

Arrange Safe and Engaging Situations. This is a time when physical activities are accelerating and will be in high gear by 24 to 26 months. Toddlers need materials, circumstances, and encouragement to do things so they will consolidate cause-effect and means-ends skills.

Caregiver	Not Yet	Occasionally	Frequently	Typically
1. Child-proofs the environment, monitors for safety issues, and attends to things that pose a hazard.	☐	☐	☐	☐
2. Provides an area that is free of dangerous obstacles so children can practice walking.	☐	☐	☐	☐
3. Sets up the environment with a variety of interesting areas for individual/small group (2 to 3 children) exploration.	☐	☐	☐	☐
4. Provides opportunities for child to explore the effects of actions.	☐	☐	☐	☐
5. Encourages the use of fingers and hands through activities such as block building.	☐	☐	☐	☐

continued

Toddlerhood

Caregiver	Not Yet	Occasionally	Frequently	Typically
6. Provides opportunities and materials that enable children to participate in imaginary play.	☐	☐	☐	☐
7. Encourages children to find objects that require searching.	☐	☐	☐	☐
8. Plays music with strong, predictable rhythms.	☐	☐	☐	☐
9. Provides an interesting/varied environment that challenges emerging motor abilities.	☐	☐	☐	☐
10. Provides objects to push and pull as walking skills develop.	☐	☐	☐	☐
11. Provides a variety of materials that encourage children to scribble.	☐	☐	☐	☐
12. Provides an obstacle course for children to negotiate to encourage the development of more refined movements, spatial awareness, coordination, and balance.	☐	☐	☐	☐
13. Plays games that include physical activity.	☐	☐	☐	☐
14. Provides materials that allow children to create through art (clay, scissors, paste, paint, crayons, markers).	☐	☐	☐	☐
15. Provides opportunities for sand and water play.	☐	☐	☐	☐

Comments:

_____

_____

_____

Make Communication a Two-Way Affair. Toddlers begin to use words to express their needs, to identify objects, and to answer simple questions. Talking to children about what is going on around them, expanding on their language, and reading with them help create a language-rich environment.

Caregiver	Not Yet	Occasionally	Frequently	Typically
16. Uses clear, developmentally appropriate language around the children.	☐	☐	☐	☐
17. Reads to the children.	☐	☐	☐	☐
18. Pairs language with daily routines and caregiving activities.	☐	☐	☐	☐
19. Responds to child's language by commenting or expanding on what the child has said.	☐	☐	☐	☐
20. Shows enthusiasm in voice and actions during reading, rhyming, and singing.	☐	☐	☐	☐
21. Tours the environment with children, describing and labeling objects.	☐	☐	☐	☐
22. Uses question words such as "who," "what," and "where" during play situations.	☐	☐	☐	☐
23. Plays turn-taking games with the children.	☐	☐	☐	☐
24. Pays attention to the child's gestures and sounds by looking and speaking to him or her.	☐	☐	☐	☐
25. Demonstrates a sense of humor, acts silly.	☐	☐	☐	☐
26. Uses words playfully or humorously, encourages child to imitate.	☐	☐	☐	☐
27. Uses puppets, flannel boards, and objects to tell stories.	☐	☐	☐	☐

Toddlerhood

continued

Caregiver	Not Yet	Occasionally	Frequently	Typically
28. Reinforces appropriate behavior (e.g., "Thank you for sharing your toy.").	☐	☐	☐	☐
29. Encourages child to talk about what he or she is doing.	☐	☐	☐	☐
30. Provides opportunities for child to follow two-step directions (e.g., "Put your cup in the sink and your napkin in the trash.").	☐	☐	☐	☐
31. Takes part in child's pretend play.	☐	☐	☐	☐
32. Repeats rhythmic, action-oriented poems.	☐	☐	☐	☐
33. Comments on children's work, play, interests, and/or products.	☐	☐	☐	☐
34. Encourages children to ask questions and answers them.	☐	☐	☐	☐
35. Encourages children to recall and share events.	☐	☐	☐	☐
36. Explains actions when demonstrating something new to a child.	☐	☐	☐	☐
37. Names items used during caregiving routines.	☐	☐	☐	☐
38. Expands a child's single-word utterances by using the word in a sentence.	☐	☐	☐	☐
39. Talks about children's actions.	☐	☐	☐	☐
40. Encourages child to participate in singing games.	☐	☐	☐	☐

Comments:

_____

_____

_____

Keep the Toddler's World Organized and Routine. Making events predictable is very important in the life of a very busy toddler. It facilitates independence, self-reliance, and a sense of security and trust.

Caregiver	Not Yet	Occasionally	Frequently	Typically
41. Has children help with daily routines.	☐	☐	☐	☐
42. Provides opportunities for children to develop functional and self-help skills.	☐	☐	☐	☐
43. Places toys and materials in the same places every day so toddlers can easily find favorite objects.	☐	☐	☐	☐
44. Provides each child with a space that is his or hers alone.	☐	☐	☐	☐
45. Ensures each child has appropriate opportunities for rest.	☐	☐	☐	☐
46. Enforces a reliable sequence for the day's activities.	☐	☐	☐	☐

Comments:

_____

_____

_____

Toddlerhood

Toys and Materials

Toys and other materials are the tools that help children construct and expand their understanding of the world around them. Carefully chosen materials will encourage children to explore their world and develop and test hypotheses about how things work. Toys and other play materials encourage large and small motor skills, problem solving, social and self-help skills, and language development.

	NO	YES
There are open-ended materials that foster creativity such as:		
1. Fat and/or chunky crayons	☐	☐
2. Finger paints	☐	☐
3. Clay, play dough	☐	☐
4. Variety of papers (construction, tissue, magazines)	☐	☐
5. Paints and variety of brushes	☐	☐
6. Glue and glue brushes	☐	☐
There are materials that foster the development of literacy skills such as:		
7. Board books	☐	☐
8. Magazines	☐	☐
9. Photo albums	☐	☐
10. Flannel board and toddler-size felt cut-outs	☐	☐
11. Variety of writing utensils	☐	☐
12. Puppets	☐	☐
13. Figurines	☐	☐
14. Old magazines	☐	☐
There are materials for constructive play such as:		
15. Blocks, bristle blocks	☐	☐
16. Large cardboard boxes	☐	☐

	NO	YES
17. Homemade blocks (from milk cartons, boxes, and/or foam cubes covered with material)	☐	☐
18. Farm sets, school sets, town sets	☐	☐
19. Cardboard tubes	☐	☐
20. Props such as people, animals, cars, trucks, trees		

There are materials for dramatic play such as:

	NO	YES
21. Variety of hats (e.g., occupation-related such as fire hats, dress-up hats, weather-related hats)	☐	☐
22. Variety of footwear (e.g., boots, sandals, shoes, high heels)	☐	☐
23. Scarves	☐	☐
24. Variety of clothing	☐	☐
25. Pots, pans, safe utensils	☐	☐
26. Dolls, stuffed toys	☐	☐

There are materials that foster the enjoyment of music and movement such as:

	NO	YES
27. Musical instruments	☐	☐
28. CDs, tapes, videos		

There are materials to encourage and support physical development such as:

	NO	YES
29. Slides	☐	☐
30. Piles of cushions for jumping on	☐	☐
31. Toys for pulling and pushing such as toy wagons, wheelbarrows, lawn mowers	☐	☐
32. Things to throw indoors such as soft or yarn balls	☐	☐
33. Things for throwing outdoors such as whiffle balls, playground balls	☐	☐

continued

Toddlerhood

	NO	YES
34. Steps (with railings)	☐	☐
35. Riding toys	☐	☐
36. Tunnels, tents	☐	☐
37. Low, soft climbing platforms	☐	☐
38. Tumbling mats	☐	☐
There are materials for sensory play such as:		
39. Sand with accessories such as small shovels, spoons, funnels, sifters, trucks, cups, containers	☐	☐
40. Water with accessories such as waterwheels, boats, cups, containers, sponges, tubing, funnels	☐	☐
41. Rice, beans, macaroni, oatmeal (with adult supervision to assure they do not find their way into children's noses)	☐	☐
42. Sensory manipulatives such as fabric, balls of yarn, sandpaper, seashells	☐	☐
There are manipulatives to encourage the development of fine motor and problem-solving skills such as:		
43. Simple puzzles (e.g., single pictures), some with knobs	☐	☐
44. Blocks	☐	☐
45. Beads for stringing	☐	☐
46. Nesting toys	☐	☐
47. Shape sorters	☐	☐
48. Busy box with things such as levers, buttons, zippers, knobs, latches, keys (attached with a chain)	☐	☐
49. Objects for banging, poking, dumping	☐	☐
50. Snap beads	☐	☐

	NO	YES
51. Table toys	☐	☐
52. Assortment of household objects such as boxes with lids, clothespins, milk jugs	☐	☐

Comments:

_____

_____

_____

Physical Attributes of the Environment

Environment plays a critical role in children's learning. The organization of space, lighting, and materials contribute to an environment that engages the senses, challenges the intellect, and promotes interaction with children and adults (Hull, Goldhaber, & Capone 2002). Quality environments are not haphazard, there is a purposeful plan for the amount and arrangement of spaces. This section of *Childmate* prompts you to think about the elements and layout of your physical space. As with all sections of *Childmate,* this section does not stand alone. As you reflect on this checklist, consider how the components relate to your space, the children who attend your program and your curricular goals. Your challenge will be to integrate this information with your own experience and knowledge as well as the information presented in other sections of *Childmate.* Remember the goal, as always, is to create an environment that motivates children to interact, explore, grow, and learn. See Appendix B for sample room arrangements and rationales for the arrangements.

	NO	YES
The facility has equipment and features such as:		
1. Carpeted and noncarpeted areas	☐	☐
2. Outdoors: small climbing equipment, slides, swings	☐	☐
3. Open shelves promoting visibility of toys (labeled with words, pictures, or symbols)	☐	☐
4. Toddler-size tables and chairs	☐	☐

continued

	NO	YES
5. Pictures near child's eye level	☐	☐
6. Visual barriers high enough for child privacy but low enough for adult supervision	☐	☐
7. Clearly differentiated, easily accessible activity areas (quiet area, crafts, exploration/discovery area, dramatic play, gross motor area)	☐	☐
8. Personal spaces for each child to "hide out"	☐	☐
9. Separate spaces for child's belongings (locker, cubby)	☐	☐
10. Pleasantly decorated areas	☐	☐
11. Wheelchair-accessible arrangements	☐	☐
12. Observation room/window	☐	☐
13. Staff space away from children	☐	☐
14. Space for meeting and talking with parents	☐	☐
15. Parent information board	☐	☐
16. Large motor equipment to invite more physical and social play	☐	☐
17. Large apparatus and materials such as boxes, big game areas to encourage pretend play	☐	☐
18. An open-modified plan that includes semiopen activity areas or pockets defined by half-walls, open archways, and windows (this appears to be most successful in supporting children's exploration and positive engagement) (Moore, 1997)	☐	☐

	NO	YES
19. Semiopen areas for easier adult monitoring of children's activity from afar, which in turn contributes to the maintenance of a calm and productive environment (Hull, Goldhaber, & Capone, 2002)	☐	☐
20. Separate activity areas, clearly defined zone, separated from other activities by space, furniture, and/or other distinct dividers (this supports easy choice making) (Gestwicki, 1999)	☐	☐

Comments:

_____

_____

_____

Toddlerhood

Do's and Don'ts

To provide quality experiences for young children, you can do the following:

1. Child-proof the environment: monitor for safety issues and attend to things that pose a hazard.

   DO

   - ☑ Remove all electrical cords from reach and cover all outlets.
   - ☑ Store all poisonous substances in a locked cabinet, out of the reach of toddlers.
   - ☑ Bolt all shelves to the wall and remove all unsteady pieces of furniture that toddlers could climb on or pull over.
   - ☑ Using locking gates to prevent toddlers from reaching dangerous areas.
   - ☑ Supervise toddlers at all times.

   DON'T Assume toddlers have a sense of safety or danger.

2. Provide an area free of dangerous obstacles so children can practice walking.

   DO

   - ☑ Provide clear paths for toddlers to maneuver through on their way to activity areas.
   - ☑ Provide open areas for gross motor practice.

   DON'T Keep toddlers in confined areas such as playpens.

3. Set up the environment with a variety of interesting areas for individual/small group (two to three children) exploration.

DO

☑ Create a number of areas (four or five, depending on the size of the group) with interesting materials and activities such as blocks, small vehicles, sensory play, book area, a housekeeping and/or baby doll area.

☑ Have duplicates, triplicates, maybe even quadruplicates of favorite play materials to encourage parallel play while respecting the fact that toddlers are not ready to share.

☑ Limit the number and duration of whole group activities.

DON'T Expect toddlers to engage in large group activities.

4. Provide opportunities for child to explore effects of actions.

DO

☑ Provide an array of materials that react to a toddler's actions such as busy boxes, musical toys, waterwheels, squeak toys.

☑ Allow children opportunities to turn doorknobs, screw and unscrew lids from plastic containers, use a pegboard, work with clay, and finger paint.

☑ Talk to toddlers about what happens when they play with materials, for example, "Look, the lights came on when you pushed that button."

☑ Make exaggerated reactions to toddler actions on materials. "Oh my, did you make that big noise happen?"

DON'T Limit toddlers' opportunities for "hands-on" exploration.

5. Encourage the use of fingers and hands through activities such as block building.

DO

☑ Provide varied opportunities for children to use hands and fingers such as dials on busy boxes, crank on jack-in-the-box, shovel and pail in sandbox, large nuts and bolts (plastic), switches and knobs, containers with lids, and finger paint.

☑ Provide items of differing size, shape, and textures that toddlers are encouraged to touch and manipulate.

☑ Talk with toddlers about the objects they are touching, giving them information about the shape, texture, and features of the object.

☑ Provide a variety of objects for children to stack (nesting objects, stacking rings, large and small blocks).

DON'T Have items available within reach that toddlers are expected not to touch.

6. Provide opportunities and materials that enable children to participate in imaginary play.

DO

- ☑ Have large, empty boxes available for toddlers to turn into caves, cars, trains, and other imaginative play spaces.

- ☑ Have hats, scarves, shoes, and large clothing available for dress-up and role-playing.

- ☑ Have an array of objects available that can be used for pretend such as tubes, boxes (of all sizes), egg cartons, pans.

DON'T Provide only realistic props in the dramatic play area.

7. Encourage children to find objects that require searching.

DO

- ☑ Play "I Spy" games, encouraging children to find objects around the environment.

- ☑ Have children help locate materials needed for daily activities.

DON'T Limit opportunities to visually explore the environment.

8. Play music with strong, predictable rhythms.

DO

- ☑ Play music with repetitive rhythms.

- ☑ Stop music during listening and have children continue the rhythm.

DON'T Limit the types of and times music is available in the environment. For example, do not play music only at naptime.

9. **Provide an interesting and varied environment that challenges emerging motor abilities.**

   DO

   ☑ Provide stimulating environment at child's level for creeping and crawling.

   ☑ Provide objects to crawl under and around.

   ☑ Provide tunnels and opened boxes.

   ☑ Provide interesting toys to crawl to.

   ☑ Provide different surfaces to crawl on.

   ☑ Hold child's arms to provide support.

   ☑ Have an interesting toy on a table or chair that the child can see only by standing.

   ☑ Have interesting sights available to standing child (fish tank, windows, pictures).

   DON'T Expect toddlers to remain in confined areas for long periods of time.

10. **Provide objects to push and pull as walking skills develop.**

    DO

    ☑ Provide objects such as large cars and buses to push.

    ☑ Provide toys that make noise when pushed and pulled.

    ☑ Provide objects that are secure to hold while pushing and pulling (carts, wagons).

    DON'T Have push and pull toys located in an area that is congested or near doors.

11. **Provide a variety of materials that encourage children to scribble.**

   DO

   - ☑ Provide a variety of writing implements (large markers, crayons, pencils).
   - ☑ Provide a variety of papers for toddlers to write on.
   - ☑ Sit with toddlers and ask them about their writing.
   - ☑ Display children's work.
   - ☑ Sit down and scribble right alongside the toddlers.
   - ☑ Talk to toddlers about the colors they are using and the types of marks they are making: "Look at that blue, curly line you just drew. It goes round and round."

   DON'T Expect toddlers to use crayons and other markers in controlled ways.

12. **Provide a safe obstacle course for children to negotiate to encourage the development of more refined movements, spatial awareness, coordination, and balance.**

   DO

   - ☑ Provide safe obstacles such as incline planes, ladder on ground, tunnel, large cardboard box (ends removed), and chairs.
   - ☑ Design obstacles in both the indoor and outdoor environments.
   - ☑ Vary the types of movements needed to negotiate the obstacle course.
   - ☑ Place cushions or mats around the course to soften a fall.

   DON'T Place a child on or in any piece of equipment that he or she is unable to negotiate on independently.

Toddlerhood

13. Play games that include physical activity.

DO

- ☑ Play games and sing songs that encourage action such as "Ring around the Rosy," "Duck, Duck, Goose," "Mother (Captain) May I?" and "Musical Chairs."
- ☑ Make obstacle courses both inside and outside.
- ☑ Use exercises as games, such as "Head, Shoulders, Knees, and Toes."
- ☑ Take nature walks.
- ☑ Dramatize stories.

DON'T Expect toddlers to sit still.

14. Provide materials that allow children to create through art.

DO

- ☑ Have crayons, markers, paste, paint, and chalk available.
- ☑ Provide large sheets of paper, cardboard, sandpaper, and construction paper.

☑ Have play dough or clay available along with an array of tools for sculpting, cutting, rolling, and shaping.

☑ Have a variety of interesting objects available for toddlers to incorporate into their artistic creations such as ribbons, sparkles, materials, and shells.

DON'T Expect children to copy adult art projects.

15. Provide opportunities for sand and water play.

DO

☑ Allow children to "paint" outdoors with large brushes and clean water.

☑ Provide various-size containers with and without spouts for water exploration.

☑ Have designated area for water play.

☑ Have box of water toys available (use domestic utensils, such as an egg beater, spatula, measuring cups, and whisk, and add soap suds or coloring).

☑ Have trucks, buckets, sifters, funnels, measuring spoons, and cups available for play.

DON'T Expect toddlers to keep sand and water in the table at all times, sensory play can be messy.

16. Use clear, developmentally appropriate language around children.

DO

- ☑ Describe what is happening in short sentences.
- ☑ Add descriptors such as words identifying size, color, sounds, and texture to toddler phrases.
- ☑ Use correct sentence structure and pronunciation when speaking with toddlers.

DON'T Use "baby talk" with toddlers.

17. Read to children.

DO

- ☑ Keep a variety of books that interest children.
- ☑ Allow children to pick stories or books.
- ☑ Read with enthusiasm, exaggeration, inflection, and emotion.
- ☑ Read to children every day.
- ☑ Point to identify objects in books.
- ☑ Acknowledge child's request to reread books.

DON'T Limit reading times to specific times of the day such as just prior to naptime.

18. Pair language with daily routines and caregiving activities.

DO

- ☑ Verbalize to children what is happening or about to happen.
- ☑ Relate events in a sequential order.
- ☑ Emphasize "key" words when verbalizing daily routines.
- ☑ Pair words with actions ("We're going around the table." "I'm brushing the doll's hair.").
- ☑ Keep explanations short and specific.

DON'T Exclude toddlers from discussions about the events that are going on around them.

19. Respond to child's language by imitating, commenting, or expanding on what he or she has said.

DO

☑ Imitate and encourage utterances.

☑ Reinforce close approximations.

☑ Provide a correct model of sounds and words.

DON'T Expect perfect language from toddlers.

20. Show enthusiasm in voice and actions during reading, rhyming, and singing.

DO

☑ Exaggerate your actions during games.

☑ Model "enjoyment" for whatever activity children are participating in.

☑ Have fun with language and language games.

DON'T Overwhelm toddlers with too much adult talk.

21. "Tour" the environment with children, describing and labeling objects.

DO

☑ Individually walk with or hold a child as you walk around the environment and name and give short explanations of objects ("This is a light switch, it turns lights off and on. Look: off, now on.").

☑ Use consistent language during explanations.

☑ Ask the child what he or she would like to explore next.

DON'T Make touring the environment a lesson that places performance demands on the child.

22. Use question words, such as "who," "what," and "where," during play situations.

DO

- ☑ Use very simple question sentences at first.
- ☑ Initially model correct responses after asking a question.

DON'T Turn question words into a test.

23. Play turn-taking games with the children.

DO

- ☑ Provide necessary wait time for turn taking.
- ☑ Be sensitive to child cues.
- ☑ Promote balance in child–caregiver interactions.
- ☑ Initially prompt a child's response if necessary.

DON'T Forget that toddlers are still egocentric or that turn taking is a new and challenging idea.

24. Pay attention to child's gestures and sounds by looking and speaking to him or her.

DO

- ☑ Look at children when you speak.
- ☑ Be aware of a child's communication for basic needs and wants (diaper change, water).
- ☑ Reinforce child utterances by responding.

DON'T Expect all a child's communications to be clear and understandable.

25. Demonstrate a sense of humor, act silly.

DO

- ☑ Dress up in different costumes (or wear clothes backward).
- ☑ Make silly faces.
- ☑ Use objects for unintended (but safe) purposes (i.e., balance a ball on your head).

DON'T Take yourself too seriously (too often).

26. **Use words playfully or humorously that encourage child to imitate you.**

DO

- ☑ Add exaggerated inflections to voice: high pitch, low pitch.
- ☑ Play vocal imitation games such as saying a silly phrase and then telling the child, "Now it's your turn."
- ☑ Repeat a child's sounds and words as if in a game.

DON'T Demand that a child speak or participate in word games.

27. **Use puppets, flannel boards, and other objects to tell children stories.**

DO

- ☑ Retell favorite stories using puppets or flannel boards.
- ☑ Ask children if they would like to participate and retell parts of favorite stories, provide props to help them remember characters and/or story events.

DON'T Turn story time into a test that requires children to remember story details.

28. Reinforce appropriate behavior.

DO

- ☑ Model and teach child to be polite.
- ☑ Model "Hi," "Good-bye," "Thank you," and "Please" in natural situations.
- ☑ Prompt child responses such as "What do we say?" and "What's the magic word?"

DON'T Expect that children will learn manners without support and reinforcement.

29. Encourage each child to talk about what he or she is doing.

DO

- ☑ Model verbalizing child's action: "You're walking up the steps."
- ☑ Ask children specific questions about their actions.
- ☑ Keep questions short and specific.
- ☑ Be an active listener: keep your attention directed to the child during verbalizations.
- ☑ Encourage the child to recall recent events.

DON'T Forget to reinforce children's attempts to describe what they are doing.

30. Provide opportunities for children to follow two-step directions.

DO

- ☑ Keep requests simple and in the same context: "Wash your hands and sit down at the table for snack." "Get your jacket and bring it to me."
- ☑ Guide or prompt child if necessary.

DON'T Overwhelm toddlers with too many directions.

31. Take part in children's pretend play.

DO

- ☑ Provide a supportive environment (toys, props).
- ☑ Help children identify salient props (a shoe for a telephone).
- ☑ Comment on children's pretend play.
- ☑ Model symbolic use of objects for children.
- ☑ Provide support for toddlers who want to join the play but may not yet know how to enter.

DON'T Dominate toddlers' play or change their play agenda.

32. Repeat rhythmic, action-oriented poems.

DO

- ☑ Teach "Itsy, Bitsy Spider" and "Where Is Thumpkin?"
- ☑ Introduce a variety of finger plays and songs with physical movements.
- ☑ Sing along and act out the songs with toddlers.

DON'T Discourage toddlers if they want to sing the same songs and finger plays over and over again.

33. Comment on children's work, play, interests, or products.

DO

☑ Provide specific, positive comments directed to the effort and specific work of the child: "You worked very hard on your drawing," or "Look at all those colors you used."

☑ Ask toddlers to tell you about their work. "Is there a story about this picture?"

☑ Display children's work around the room, making sure it is at the children's level.

DON'T Name a child's picture before checking with the child.

34. Encourage children to ask questions and answer the questions they ask.

DO

☑ Encourage children to be inquisitive about the world around them by modeling the behavior. For example, on a walk outdoors speculate with the children about ideas such as, "I wonder which will make a bigger splash, this rock or this leaf?"

☑ Read children's facial expressions, "Jake, you look as if you have a question about this."

☑ Ask children if they have any questions or ideas they are wondering about.

DON'T Ignore children's questions or wonderings.

35. Encourage children to recall and share events.

DO

☑ Talk with children about recent events such as a trip to Grandma's house, a birthday, or going to the grocery store.

☑ Ask children open-ended questions about what they did or enjoyed about a recent event.

☑ Help children find the words to talk about the event.

DON'T Tell children about something they have done without incorporating them and their perspective into the telling.

36. Explain actions when demonstrating something to a child.

DO

☑ When teaching new skills, verbalize what you are doing.

☑ Pair words with actions.

DON'T Overwhelm toddlers with long descriptions.

37. Name items used in caregiving routines.

DO

☑ Talk to children by naming everyday objects used in daily activities.

☑ When naming objects, group them into categories (spoon and fork, cup and plate, car and road).

DON'T Test the child by asking him or her to name objects.

Toddlerhood

38. **Expand children's single-word utterances by using them in simple sentences.**

   DO

   ☑ Verify a child's intent in using a single-word utterance by using the word in a sentence for the child (Child: "Water." Teacher: "Let's go get some water.")

   ☑ Enthusiastically reinforce the child's usage of words.

   ☑ Closely attend to the child's pattern of speech and say the word correctly in a short sentence.

   DON'T Correct everything a child says.

39. **Talk about a child's actions ("You're crawling under the chair.").**

   DO

   ☑ Pair your language with the child's actions

   ☑ Have the child repeat "action" words while doing the action (for an older toddler).

   ☑ Use enthusiasm in speech-emphasizing "action" words.

   DON'T Ignore what children are doing.

40. **Encourage children to participate in singing games.**

   DO

   ☑ Use singing throughout daily activities.

   ☑ Make up songs for daily activities (i.e., "Today we're going to paint a picture, paint a picture, paint a picture.").

   ☑ Present a variety of children's songs to youngsters.

   DON'T Demand that children engage in singing games (many toddlers will enjoy participating simply by listening and watching).

41. Have children help with daily routines.

DO

☑ Provide a sense of responsibility by having children retrieve items, set up for activities, and clean up.

☑ Reinforce child participation.

DON'T Expect toddlers to do things perfectly.

42. Provide opportunities for children to develop functional and self-help skills.

DO

☑ Create play settings where children can demonstrate use of objects in their settings (feeding doll, bathing doll).

☑ Model object functions (use of soap, cup, spoon).

☑ Encourage brushing and combing of hair and brushing of teeth.

☑ Encourage washing of face and hands, self-feeding, and taking off coat or jacket.

☑ Encourage children to complete simple tasks independently.

DON'T Forget to reinforce toddlers' attempts at independence and taking care of themselves.

Toddlerhood

43. Place toys and materials in the same places every day so toddlers can easily find favorite objects.

DO

- ☑ Have designated areas for materials so that items such as blocks, sand and water, and manipulatives are always found in the same place.

- ☑ Label shelves with pictures and words so that toddlers have clues for where things can be found and where they belong during cleanup.

DON'T Constantly rearrange the environment. (This makes life challenging for toddlers, who are just beginning to understand how to appropriately take control of themselves and the world around them.)

44. Include a variety of materials in each play area so that children with differing abilities and interests can play together.

DO

- ☑ Examine the materials included in each play area from the perspective of each child in the room.

- ☑ Adapt any materials to assure that a child with a disability or challenge can participate in the play area.

- ☑ Talk to children about the play areas and the materials they would like to find there.

DON'T Expect children to conform to adult expectations of how a particular play area should be used.

45. Provide each child with a space that is his or hers alone.

DO

- ☑ Provide each child with a cubby that is his or her own space.

- ☑ Label each child's private space with his or her picture and name.

DON'T Change a child's space.

46. Assure that each child has appropriate opportunities for rest.

DO

☑ Provide a time and place for each child to have an undisturbed nap.

☑ Provide quiet areas of the room where children can cuddle with a book or small toys and rest (rather than sleep).

☑ Provide a balance of active and quiet activities throughout the day.

DON'T Have naptime be the only opportunity for rest.

47. Have a reliable sequence to the day's activities.

DO

☑ Have a daily schedule that is predictable so that toddlers are able to develop an expectation of what will happen next.

☑ Make a picture schedule and post it at toddler level so that children can check on the events of the day.

☑ Provide warnings for transitions.

DON'T Be rigid about the time of activities; take your cue from the children. (Some days playtime may go on for 40 minutes, while other days it may go on for 20 minutes. Just be consistent with the sequence of activities.)

Toddlerhood

For additional information on appraising quality child care, visit our Web site at http://www.earlychilded.delmar.com

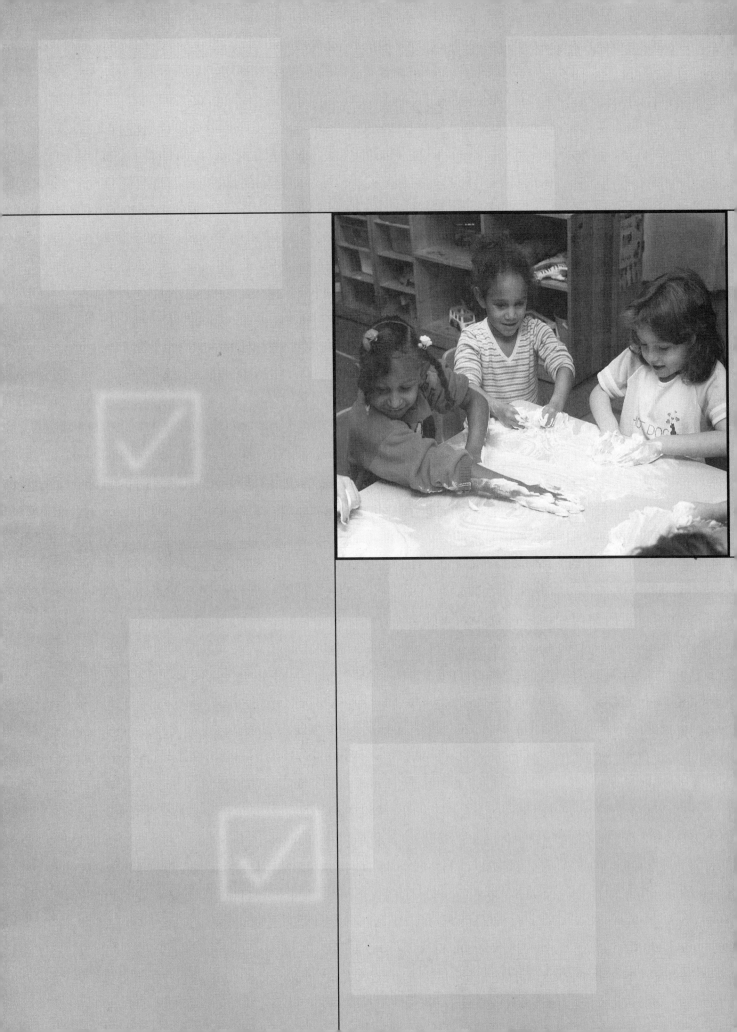

Section 3

Preschool Years
(36 to 60 Months)

Richie (41 months) was delighted to see the new setup at the water table. There was a funnel, some tubing, a waterwheel, and differently sized cups for filling and dumping. Richie loved the water table, spending long periods of time pouring water into the waterwheel and funnels often placed around its sides. Today Richie's teacher (Eileen) decided to challenge his understanding of these familiar objects. She wanted to see how Richie approached a new configuration of familiar objects. She set up the waterwheel in such a way that it would turn only if water was poured into the funnel at the edge of the water table. Eileen watched as Richie approached the waterwheel in the

usual way, pouring cup after cup of water into the top. The new setup, however, would not let the waterwheel go around. Perhaps thinking that the wheel was stuck, Richie moved the wheel by hand, dumped water in with great force, and even poured water with one hand while moving the wheel with the other. None of his strategies worked.

Eileen, who was nearby watching, noted each of Richie's strategies. She also noted the amount of time Richie persisted at this task. After 2 or 3 minutes, she decided to join him. She began by very quietly filling the funnel and watching as the water traveled down the tube and into the top of the waterwheel, turning the wheel as it passed through the opening at the top. Richie was clearly surprised to see that the wheel was working, and once again he tried his old strategies. Eileen continued playing at the funnel end of the table, carrying on a conversation about their parallel play, but never revealing the answer. Richie tried a number of new strategies such as using Eileen's cup (maybe the magic was in the cup) and moving to Eileen's side of the table. After about 20 minutes, Richie took Eileen's cup, filled it, and dumped it into the funnel. Delighted at the result, he turned to Eileen and simply said, "I did it."

Developmental Overview of Preschool Years (36 to 60 Months)

For many who work with preschool-age children, the descriptor *independent learners* rings true. At this age, children formulate hypotheses about how things work and spend considerable time testing and retesting those hypotheses. Preschoolers are developing the social skills necessary to play in small groups; becoming competent in daily living and personal care skills; becoming aware of more than they can express; and refining fine and gross motor skills. In short, preschoolers are physical beings, whose interactions with people, events, and objects enable them to create new understandings about the world around them. The curiosity evident in the perpetual questioning of toddlers now explodes into a desire to find answers independently. It is not unusual to find a group of preschool youngsters constructing fairly complex activities for answering "burning" questions. Because the preschool years include a longer time span than infancy or toddlerhood, it is difficult to talk about the accomplishments of this period. Three-year-olds understand and interact with the world differently than four-year-olds, who themselves are distinctively different than five-year-olds. The course of development during the preschool years can, however, be discussed in terms of four significant themes: establishing friendships, self-directed learning, active exploration, and discovering the power of words.

Are You My Friend?

Spending time with peers is priority one for most preschool youngsters. They enjoy each other's company, invest enormous amounts of time and energy understanding friends and friendships, and become increasingly competent play partners (Gestwicki, 1999). In addition, preschoolers' new verbal abilities allow them to regulate their own behavior and the behavior of others in less aggressive, and more friendly, ways. Play provides a rich context for observing the growing social competence of children during the preschool years. While many three-year-olds entering the preschool years engage in only onlooker play (watching the play of others without attempting to join them), most will quickly pass through

the stages of parallel play (engaging in similar kinds of play near another child without interaction) and associative play (playing together, with brief episodes of interactive play). They emerge as a "cooperative player" capable of selecting playmates and developing plans for play. As children become self-assured and able to cooperate with peers, their games become more organized and involve turn taking and rules. By five years of age, most children have become competent social beings who value and nurture special friendships.

Self-Directed Learners

Preschoolers are full of ideas and the energy to implement them. They work alone, in pairs, and in groups. While they love sharing their ideas and discoveries with adults, preschoolers are far less dependent on adult attention and assistance than toddlers. The opening story of Richie at the water table is a wonderful example of a preschooler's approach to play and learning. Richie approached the water table with a plan and an expectation. When the play materials did not work as expected, he used a number of strategies to adjust his play. His teacher's plan and behavior reflected her knowledge of preschool-age children. Understanding that preschoolers want to discover new ideas for themselves, she did not tell Richie how to use the new setup. Instead, she played alongside him, and

her play gave him new information. Over the course of his play, Richie developed and tested a number of hypotheses. Finally, he was able to make the new setup work. A preschooler's own experimentation and discovery are indeed wonderful.

Physically Active Beings

In addition to actively exploring materials and testing hypotheses, preschoolers are physically active. As toddlerhood draws to an end, most children have mastered large motor skills. What they have not yet mastered are coordination and agility. During the preschool years, increased coordination allows children to be on the move. Their increasing attention span allows them to stick with an activity until mastered. As a result, gross motor skills expand greatly during the preschool years, children learn to skip, jump, climb, and throw various objects overhand. During the later preschool years, as motor movements become smooth, preschoolers learn to ride bikes, scooters, and skateboards, pull wagons, and maneuver their way across monkey bars.

Fine motor skills are also refined during the preschool years. For some, handedness may emerge at this time, although for others, it may not develop until kindergarten. During this period, children cut with scissors, color, and copy simple geometric shapes. Their fine motor skills

Preschool Years

enable them to copy letters, draw pictures, and manipulate small objects to create interesting sculptures and representations of objects in their environment. The combination of their fine motor skills, language abilities, and need for exploration allows them to express their understanding of the world in new and exciting ways (e.g., writing books, stories, making signs, creating three-dimensional representations of their discoveries).

Discovering the Power of Words

Intellectual and linguistic abilities expand dramatically during the preschool years. In general, preschoolers become more social and less egocentric. They begin to form concepts about their environment and world and are able to communicate those discoveries to both peers and adults. What they perceive generally dominates their judgment, although magic and fantasy are increasing fixtures in their everyday world. In the early preschool years, children ask endless questions, begin to generalize, and are highly dramatic and imaginative. By age five they know over 2,000 words, can retell stories, show a keen interest in words, and begin to understand the difference between truth and lies, fact and fiction. By age five, speech should generally be grammatically correct. A five-year-old can follow three-step commands, define objects by their use, and understand concepts such as position and difference. These changes are the result of interactions with people, events, and objects. The sense of autonomy children develop during the toddler years is expressed as a sense of "initiative" as preschoolers. During the preschool years, children learn to be both leaders and followers. They accept, and even seek out, increased responsibility. Preschoolers express their sense of initiative through their pretend play, inventing, creating, taking risks, and playing with others (Gestwicki, 1999). As preschoolers initiate their own activities and enjoy their accomplishments, they demonstrate greater and greater confidence in their own abilities.

Preschool Years

Guiding Principles for Supporting Optimal Development in Group Care Settings

Create an Environment Suitable for Exploration and Hypothesis Testing

Busy hands, busy bodies, and busy minds make for very busy settings. Preschoolers pose exciting challenges for caregivers! The key to responding effectively to these challenges is designing environments that allow children to be active participants. Preschoolers are capable of deciding what materials they want and how they want to use them. They thrive on discovering new relationships between familiar materials and exploring ideas in new ways. As children become involved with materials like clay, finger paint, water, sand, flour, blocks, and manipulatives, they make discoveries about physical properties and their own ability to manipulate materials, express their ideas, and solve problems. For example, discovering the relationship between shaving cream and paint

is both interesting and logical and can lead to new understandings of color and texture. An interest in fairies may provoke months of play designing fairy houses, baking fairy food, creating fairy playgrounds, and writing fairy books. The observant caregiver will support this play by providing a variety of materials, asking authentic questions, and provoking new ideas. Open-ended materials that bring the preschooler physically into the task and encourage the ability to look beyond the obvious are key for the development of flexible thinking. Activities that establish a solid knowledge base encourage exploration.

Encourage Initiative and Self-Reliance

Foster active learning, independence, and initiative by organizing the environment and establishing routines that lead to success. The ability to be self-directed and make choices is more likely to develop when the choices are clear and materials are provided in sufficient quantity. Open-ended materials are also important means to provide an atmosphere where children express their own interest, take initiative, and develop strategies for testing their hypotheses and examining their ideas. Materials that have no right or wrong answers and are process oriented rather than product oriented are essential tools for original thinking, creativity, and self-direction. Clay, paints, paper, glue, sand, and blocks encourage children to be creative. Seek out interests of individual children and provide them with choices within the environment and routines that enable them to follow their passions and examine their beliefs. Encouraging preschoolers to do as much for themselves as possible is essential, especially during routines (e.g., snack, bathroom, entering class, and cleanup) and play time.

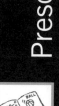

Communication Is the Name of the Game for Preschoolers

Preschool children need to thoughtfully interact with the world in order to understand it. They may not always have the words necessary to do this. You can facilitate the development of more complex language by reading stories, describing what the children are doing, and answering questions. Through verbal interactions with adults, children develop greater competence in interpreting their actions and thus develop a more complete understanding of the world.

A child acquires language to express what he or she already knows nonlinguistically. Concepts become the prerequisites to functional language development. Language will build on the cognitive base that develops through the child's interaction with the environment and his or her internal interpretation of the experiences that occur during this interaction. The capacity to communicate is an essential skill, which enables children to express what they want and need as well as to develop friendships, ask questions, and describe experiences. Preschoolers need to be provided with numerous opportunities to practice communicating. When teachers do most of the talking or when there are rules that consistently require children to be silent, children are deprived of the opportunity to practice these critical skills (Hull, Goldhaber, & Capone, 2002).

Play Is the Rule of the Day

Play is a vital aspect of the normal developmental process. It is the avenue to self-discovery and environmental awareness. In play, children engage in a process of exploration and trial-and-error hypothesis testing, without fear of failure, which provides the foundation for language, cognition, and socialization. Play and learning are not opposites, but rather two parts of the important process of understanding self, other, and the world. Cognitive skills develop as a reflection of play skills, making abstraction and representation (academics) useful skills for interaction with the world. A white shirt and wooden spoon can transport the playful child into the world of medicine. Taking temperatures, examining ears and throats, and even a tonsillectomy may become understandable, rather than threatening. Letters and numbers combine to form symbols that represent familiar persons, places, and things and allow children to express ideas in new and permanent ways. Caregivers can facilitate play by having appropriate activities, toys, and materials available in all areas of the room, providing extended periods of time for play and exploration, and encouraging children to expand upon their play ideas by providing props, organizing materials, and narrating (and not dominating children's play).

It is important to plan outdoor play experiences as carefully as indoor play environments. In addition to providing opportunities for bike riding, running, jumping, and sliding, the out of doors can be a rich context for dramatic play, art, music, and literacy.

Support the Development of Emotional Control

Preschoolers are physical beings, but they are beginning to understand the viewpoint of others and how their actions affect others. They also may become easily frustrated, so caregivers must be proactive. Start by showing each child that he or she is special and that you are interested in his or her activities and conversations. It is also important to treat each child with respect by listening to what each one says, showing enthusiasm for what each one does, and providing consistency in your actions. Behaviors that interfere with the learning of the child and others can be minimized by establishing routines, with a few clear rules that are consistently adhered to, and careful planning of daily activities. Provide encouragement and praise to children who share and take turns. Closely monitor situations before they get out of hand and encourage children to use words rather than physical actions when trying to solve problems.

Checklists

Caregiver Behaviors

The behaviors of caregivers are key to quality experiences for young children. Caregivers who participate in a cycle of inquiry that includes observation, reflection, and the creation of responsive learning opportunities create settings that support young children to become alert, thoughtful, and confident youngsters who come up with interesting ideas, problems, and questions. Observation, reflection, adaptation, and planning are essential tools for responding to, and promoting, a young child's curiosity. They are the keys to responsive caregiving.

The following caregiver behaviors have been shown to be effective strategies for accomplishing these goals. Check the appropriate box.

Create an Environment Suitable for Exploration and Hypothesis Testing. Arrange the environment to promote exploration and discovery. Preschoolers love to be actively involved in activities, make discoveries, solve problems, and express their own ideas.

Caregiver	Not Yet	Occasionally	Frequently	Typically
1. Encourages self-directed problem solving and experimentation.	☐	☐	☐	☐
2. Provides opportunities for children to explore the physical properties of a wide variety of objects.	☐	☐	☐	☐
3. Provides opportunities for children to formulate ideas (hypotheses) about how things work and how different objects and events may be related to each other.	☐	☐	☐	☐
4. Asks questions that challenge children to think about what they are doing in new ways.	☐	☐	☐	☐
5. Encourages experimentation and creativity rather than imitation.	☐	☐	☐	☐

Caregiver	Not Yet	Occasionally	Frequently	Typically
6. Encourages children to make plans and initiate their own activities.	☐	☐	☐	☐

Comments:

_____

_____

_____

Encourage Initiative and Self-Reliance. Design situations to promote initiative, self-help, and success. You can foster independence and encourage initiative by organizing the environment and establishing routines that enable children to be successful in daily routines (e.g., snack, getting ready to go home) and in play.

Caregiver	Not Yet	Occasionally	Frequently	Typically
7. Encourages children to dress themselves.	☐	☐	☐	☐
8. Plans for transitions between activities and prepares children by telling or signaling about an upcoming transition.	☐	☐	☐	☐
9. Establishes daily routines for children.	☐	☐	☐	☐
10. Encourages children to clean up after themselves, putting things back where they belong.	☐	☐	☐	☐
11. Encourages children to make choices and requests during snack time.	☐	☐	☐	☐
12. Encourages children to follow social rules in work and play.	☐	☐	☐	☐
13. Provides opportunities to practice and understand good safety procedures such as when boarding, riding, or leaving a bus.	☐	☐	☐	☐

continued

Preschool Years

Caregiver	Not Yet	Occasionally	Frequently	Typically
14. Encourages the expression of preferences for activities and materials.	☐	☐	☐	☐
15. Encourages children to participate in simple group problem-solving situations.	☐	☐	☐	☐

Comments:

_____

_____

_____

Communication is the Name of the Game for Preschoolers. **Make child-to-child and child-to-caregiver communication rewarding and expected. The capacity to communicate is an essential skill that enables children to express what they want and need as well as to develop friendships, ask questions, and describe experiences. Preschoolers need to be provided with numerous and varied opportunities to practice communicating.**

Caregiver	Not Yet	Occasionally	Frequently	Typically
16. Encourages the use of "body language" to add expression or clarify meaning.	☐	☐	☐	☐
17. Helps children learn and use new words.	☐	☐	☐	☐
18. Uses size-related words to describe objects and encourages children to do the same.	☐	☐	☐	☐
19. Uses language for children to imitate.	☐	☐	☐	☐
20. Provides activities to develop language and literacy through meaningful experience.	☐	☐	☐	☐
21. Creates learning centers that encourage children to explore and discuss ideas and concepts in small groups.	☐	☐	☐	☐

Caregiver	Not Yet	Occasionally	Frequently	Typically
22. Participates in discussions with children about their discoveries, explorations, and interests.	☐	☐	☐	☐
23. Encourages children to contribute to group discussions.	☐	☐	☐	☐
24. Encourages conversation between children.	☐	☐	☐	☐
25. Encourages children to use their language for expressing feelings, ideas, and needs.	☐	☐	☐	☐
26. Reads to children.	☐	☐	☐	☐
27. Participates in discussions about books with children.	☐	☐	☐	☐
28. Encourages children to read.	☐	☐	☐	☐
29. Sets up a writing center.	☐	☐	☐	☐
30. Provides opportunities for children to copy names, letters, and other meaningful words.	☐	☐	☐	☐

Comments:

_____

_____

_____

Preschool Years

Play is the Rule of the Day. Promote play and preschool fun. Play is a vital aspect of the normal developmental process. It is the avenue to self-discovery and environmental awareness. In play, children engage in a process of exploration and trial-and-error hypothesis testing that provides the foundation for language, cognition, and socialization.

Caregiver	Not Yet	Occasionally	Frequently	Typically
31. Provides a variety of "play spaces" so that children can select from a number of different play options (e.g., pretend play, dramatic play, dance and movement).	☐	☐	☐	☐
32. Encourages games and other play that include physical activity.	☐	☐	☐	☐
33. Provides social opportunities to meet and play with other children and adults.	☐	☐	☐	☐
34. Shows interest and enjoyment in children by listening to music, playing games, or dancing with them.	☐	☐	☑	☐
35. Includes a variety of materials in each play area so that children with differing abilities and interests can play together.	☐	☐	☐	☐
36. Observes and records what children do during play.	☐	☐	☐	☐
37. Provides children with at least 35 to 40 minutes of uninterrupted, child-directed choice time daily.	☐	☐	☐	☐

Comments:

_____

_____

_____

Support the Development of Emotional Control. Model and encourage sensitivity to the problems and feelings of others. Preschoolers are beginning to understand the viewpoints of others and how their actions affect others. Be proactive and show children that they are special by expressing interest in their activities and conversations.

Caregiver	Not Yet	Occasionally	Frequently	Typically
38. Encourages children to problem solve during play and group activities.	☐	☐	☐	☐
39. Encourages the expression of feelings, including those of a more abstract nature.	☐	☐	☐	☐
40. Uses guidance techniques: models and encourages expected behavior to help the development of self-control.	☐	☐	☐	☐
41. Provides affection and support; comforts children when they cry and reassures them when they are fearful.	☐	☐	☐	☐
42. Offers experiences to alleviate children's fears.	☐	☐	☐	☐
43. Structures activities that require sharing.	☐	☐	☐	☐
44. Encourages children to participate in simple group problem-solving situations.	☐	☐	☐	☐
45. Spends one-on-one time with each child each day.	☐	☐	☐	☐

Comments:

_____

_____

_____

Preschool Years

Toys and Materials

Toys and other materials are the tools that help children construct and expand their understanding of the world around them. Carefully chosen materials will encourage children to develop and test hypotheses about how the world works. Open-ended materials foster creativity and allow children to express personal interests and approaches to learning.

	NO	YES
There are open-ended materials that foster creativity such as:		
1. Markers, pencils, pens, crayons, pastels	☐	☐
2. Tempera paints, watercolors	☐	☐
3. Clay, play dough	☐	☐
4. Construction paper, writing paper	☐	☐
5. Papier-mâché	☐	☐
6. Scissors	☐	☐
7. Glue, paste, sparkles	☐	☐
8. Finger paints	☐	☐
There are materials that foster the development of literacy skills such as:		
9. A variety of different types of books (e.g., storybooks, wordless books, concept books)	☐	☐
10. Notebooks	☐	☐
11. Individual journal for each child	☐	☐
12. Typewriter/computer	☐	☐
13. Variety of writing utensils	☐	☐
14. Puppets	☐	☐
15. Flannel board	☐	☐
16. Photo albums	☐	☐
17. Figurines	☐	☐
18. Old magazines	☐	☐

	NO	YES
There are materials for constructive play:		
19. Wooden blocks, plastic connecting blocks, bristle blocks	☐	☐
20. Manipulatives such as snap beads, nesting toys	☐	☐
21. Beads for stringing	☐	☐
22. Farm sets, school sets, town sets	☐	☐
23. Cardboard tubes	☐	☐
24. Props such as people, animals, cars, trucks, trees	☐	☐
There are materials for dramatic play:		
25. Variety of hats (e.g., occupation-related, such as fire hats, dress-up hats, weather-related hats)	☐	☐
26. Variety of footwear (e.g., boots, sandals, shoes, high heels)	☐	☐
27. Scarves	☐	☐
28. Variety of clothing	☐	☐
29. Pots, pans, safe utensils	☐	☐
30. Dolls, stuffed toys	☐	☐
There are materials that foster the enjoyment of music and movement:		
31. CDs, tapes, videos	☐	☐
32. Musical instruments	☐	☐
There are materials that facilitate scientific investigations:		
33. Magnifying glasses	☐	☐
34. Eye droppers	☐	☐
35. Tools for measuring (measuring spoons and cups, scales for weighing, rulers)	☐	☐

continued

Preschool Years

	NO	YES
There are materials to encourage and support physical development:		
36. Slides	☐	☐
37. Piles of cushions for jumping on	☐	☐
38. Toys for pulling and pushing such as wagons	☐	☐
39. Things to throw indoors such as soft balls and yarn balls	☐	☐
40. Things for throwing outdoors, such as whiffle balls, playground balls	☐	☐
41. Jungle gym	☐	☐
42. Pedal vehicles	☐	☐
43. Tumbling mats	☐	☐
There are materials for sensory play:		
44. Sand	☐	☐
45. Water	☐	☐
46. Rice, beans	☐	☐
There are some additional materials such as:		
47. Board games (e.g., matching games, memory games, games with simple rules such as Chutes and Ladders™)	☐	☐
48. Puzzles	☐	☐
49. Different-size boxes for pretending and creating	☐	☐
50. Theme boxes that include an array of materials, books, and activities related to a specific theme such as restaurant, post office, grocery store	☐	☐

Comments:

_____

_____

_____

Physical Attributes of the Environment

Environment plays a critical role in children's learning. The organization of space, light, and materials contributes to an environment that engages the senses, challenges the intellect, and promotes interaction with children and adults (Hull, Goldhaber, & Capone, 2002). This section of *Childmate* prompts you to think about the elements and layout of your physical space. As with all sections of *Childmate*, this section does not stand alone. As you reflect on this checklist, consider how the components relate to your space, the children who attend your program and your curricula goals. Your challenge will be to integrate this information with your own experience and knowledge as well as the information presented in other sections of *Childmate*. Remember the goal, as always, is to create an environment that motivates children to interact, explore, grow, and learn. See Appendix B for sample room arrangements and rationales for the arrangements.

The facility has:	NO	YES
1. Carpeted and noncarpeted areas	☐	☐
2. Outdoors: small climbing equipment, slides, swings	☐	☐
3. Open shelves for visibility of toys (labeled with words, pictures, or symbols)	☐	☐
4. Child-size tables and chairs	☐	☐
5. Pictures and bulletin boards near child's eye level	☐	☐
6. Visual barriers high enough for child privacy but low enough for adult supervision	☐	☐
7. Clearly differentiated, easily accessible activity areas (quiet area, crafts, exploration/ discovery area, dramatic play, gross motor area)	☐	☐
8. Personal spaces for each child to "hide out"	☐	☐
9. Separate spaces for child's belongings (locker, cubby)	☐	☐
10. Appropriately, pleasantly decorated	☐	☐
11. Wheelchair-accessible arrangements	☐	☐

continued

Preschool Years

	NO	YES
12. Observation room or window	☐	☐
13. Staff space away from children	☐	☐
14. Space for meeting and talking with parents	☐	☐
15. Parent information board	☐	☐
A few guidelines for consideration:		
16. Large motor equipment invites more physical and social play.	☐	☐
17. Make-believe is more likely to happen when children are playing with large apparatus (Smith & Connolly, 1980).	☐	☐
18. The amount of space you have and how you arrange it affects children's behavior (Hull, Goldhaber, & Capone, 2002).	☐	☐
19. An open-modified plan that includes semiopen activity areas or pockets defined by half-walls, open archways, and windows, appears to be most successful in supporting children's exploration and positive engagement (Moore, 1997).	☐	☐
20. Semiopen areas make it easier for adults to monitor children's activity from afar, which in turn contributes to the maintenance of a calm and productive environment (Hull, Goldhaber, & Capone 2002).	☐	☐
21. Each activity needs to be set up in its own, clearly defined zone separated from other activities by space, furniture, or other distinct dividers (this supports easy choice making) (Gestwicki, 1999).	☐	☐

Comments:

_____

_____

_____

Do's and Don'ts

To provide quality experiences for young children, you can do the following:

1. ## Encourage self-directed problem solving and experimentation.

    DO

    ☑ Help children to talk through and think of creative solutions to problems (e.g., "It is raining, so we can't have our picnic outside. What can we do?").

    ☑ Involve children in simple experiments like seeing whether objects will sink or float in water.

    ☑ Ask children to make predictions. "What will happen if _____?"

    DON'T Do everything for children when making their own decisions would provide a learning experience.

2. ## Provide opportunities for children to explore the physical properties of a wide variety of objects.

    DO

    ☑ Provide collections of objects including objects that are similar and different on a variety of dimensions, such as size, shape, texture, and function.

    ☑ Encourage children to organize objects by characteristics. Objects can be organized in baskets, boxes, or on shelves, so that the object remains in sight and the child can examine his or her work.

    DON'T Discourage children from manipulating objects by various properties.

Preschool Years

3. Provide opportunities for children to formulate ideas (hypotheses) about how things work and how different objects and events may be related to each other.

   DO

   ☑ Take pictures of children's explorations and discoveries. Write down their descriptions of what is happening and what they have learned.

   ☑ Ask children questions about what they are exploring to prompt them to make mental connections between what they already know and what they are learning.

   DON'T Tell children what is happening and why. Don't correct immature understandings of events.

4. Ask questions that challenge children to think about what they are doing in new ways.

   DO

   ☑ Ask questions that prompt children to consider alternatives, such as, "How do you think that would work if you used paper instead of clay?"

   ☑ Ask questions that challenge children to think about what they are doing such as, "Why did you use that piece?"

   ☑ Ask questions that prompt children to reflect on what is happening such as, "Why do you think the play dough is now purple?"

   DON'T Limit your use of questions to quizzing children about concepts such as color, amount, or labels.

5. Encourage experimentation and creativity rather than imitation.

DO

☑ Provide materials that are open ended, have no right or wrong answer, and can be used in a variety of ways.

☑ Talk to children about how they used the materials and what they were thinking rather than asking them to name their product.

DON'T Expect all children to make the same product or copy an adult model.

Preschool Years

6. Encourage children to make plans and initiate their own activities.

DO

☑ Observe children's play to gather information about the types of materials they enjoy, types of activities they prefer, and ideas they are interested in.

☑ Set out materials that you know the children are interested in.

☑ Ask children about their plans. "What are you planning to do?" "What materials will you need?" "How will you begin your plan?"

DON'T Get so caught up in teacher plans and activities that it becomes difficult to adapt in response to children's plans.

7. Encourage children to dress themselves.

DO

☑ Allow children to put on and take off their own coats, boots, and other outerwear when leaving or entering the building, providing the least amount of help needed.

☑ Provide dolls and doll clothing or dress-up clothing with zippers, snaps, buttons, and buckles.

DON'T Dress children who can dress themselves (even if time is an issue.)

8. Plan for transitions between activities and prepare children by telling or signaling about upcoming transitions.

DO

☑ Warn children of activity changes several minutes before they will occur (e.g., "You have five more minutes to play and then it will be time to clean up.").

☑ Teach children a signal for changing to a different activity (e.g., turning off the lights, playing a tune on the piano, ringing a small bell, clapping your hands, singing a familiar song).

DON'T Abruptly change activities without providing prior warning to children.

9. Establish several daily routines for children.

DO

☑ Have a specific time for routines like snack, outside play, nap or rest time, and other classroom routines.

☑ Keep your schedule consistent from day to day.

DON'T Allow random decision making to drive the day's activities.

10. Encourage children to clean up after themselves and put things back where they belong.

DO

☑ Have a classroom rule about cleanup (e.g., everyone helps clean up, cleanup occurs at a certain time or after each activity).

☑ Assign cleanup helpers for different tasks and give each child a turn at helping.

☑ Praise all attempts to help with the cleanup process.

DON'T Make it difficult for children to help with cleanup.

11. Encourage children to make choices and requests during snack time.

DO

- ☑ Prompt children to request items during snack (e.g., "What do you want?" "You want more juice. Say more juice.").
- ☑ Give children the items they request promptly after they have requested them.
- ☑ Allow children to use a variety of requesting behaviors such as a head nod, pointing, smiling.
- ☑ Praise children who ask for items.

DON'T Deny snack to children who are unable or unwilling to request a snack.

12. Encourage children to follow social rules in work and play situations.

DO

- ☑ Have children participate in establishing classroom rules.
- ☑ Remind children regularly about the class rules and the consequences.
- ☑ When a child breaks a rule, tell him or her which rule has been broken and the consequence, then enforce the consequence.

DON'T Have a large number of rules for children to remember and follow.

13. Provide opportunities to practice and understand good safety procedures such as when boarding, riding, or leaving a bus.

DO

- ☑ Talk about, and practice, following safety procedures for the bus.
- ☑ Tell children simply why the procedures are important (e.g., "We stay in our seat so we won't get hurt.").
- ☑ Practice and have parents practice procedures with children.

DON'T Expect children to master skills without modeling by adults and time to practice.

14. **Encourage the expression of preferences for activities and materials.**

DO

- ☑ Allow time in the day for free-play choices, allowing children to choose where they want to play.

- ☑ Allow children to decide how they will use the materials that are available.

- ☑ Allow children to choose between two or more activities (e.g., sand or water table).

DON'T Don't limit children's opportunities for making choices throughout the day and in different types of situations.

15. **Encourage children to participate in simple group problem-solving activities.**

DO

- ☑ Provide children with a variety of open-ended materials.

- ☑ Expect children to use their existing skills to solve new problems.

- ☑ Encourage children to "try out" their ideas.

- ☑ Encourage children to talk with each other about their ideas for completing different tasks or using different materials.

DON'T Provide quick answers to "problems" that children encounter.

Preschool Years

16. Encourage the children to use body language to add expression and/or clarify their meaning.

DO

☑ Use your own arms, feet, hands, shoulders, and facial expressions, along with your speech.

☑ Look at pictures of people or watch people on TV with the sound turned off. Talk about the way people move when they talk and what they might be feeling or saying.

☑ Say poems or sing songs that have motions and exaggerated facial expressions.

DON'T Discourage children from demonstrating the use of nonverbal signals.

17. Help children to learn and use new words.

DO

☑ Help each child make a personal dictionary that includes words he or she knows and examples (pictures of the words).

☑ Define new words as they appear in context (e.g., "Then they husked the corn. Husking is taking the parts that are like leaves off the corncob.").

☑ Expand on what the child says: add new words, repeat the child's statement using correct grammar, and add descriptive words.

DON'T Make language and literacy a didactic activity.

18. Use size-related words to describe objects and encourage children to do the same.

DO

☑ Use size words to describe common objects ("What a huge tree!" "That's a tiny dog.").

☑ Give children opportunities to categorize objects by size. Provide various size words to label categories (e.g., humorous, huge, tiny, teensy-weensy, big, large, small).

DON'T Inhibit children's opportunities to experiment with properties of size.

19. Use language for children to imitate.

DO

☑ Talk about the child's daily activities.

☑ Use proper grammar

☑ Speak clearly and in a normal tone of voice.

DON'T Use baby talk.

20. Provide activities to develop language and literacy through meaningful experience.

DO

☑ Read to, and have children read, stories, poems, and words to songs.

☑ Encourage children to dictate and read their own group or individual stories.

☑ Take field trips. Before going, talk about what you might see, and after returning, write and read about the experience. Write a group (or individual) thank-you letter to the field trip host.

DON'T Expect children to develop skills without an array of rich experience.

21. Create learning centers that encourage children to explore and discuss ideas and concepts in small groups.

DO

- ☑ Set up learning centers that reflect children's interests (e.g., water, plants, horses, fairies).

- ☑ Provide a variety of materials at the center that encourage conversation, such as books, pictures, manipulatives.

- ☑ Talk with the children about what they are exploring and thinking about; encourage them to share their ideas with each other.

- ☑ Create opportunities for children to tell each other about things that are happening in the learning center.

DON'T Use this as an opportunity to do direct teaching on a topic.

22. Participate in discussions with children about their discoveries, explorations, and interests.

DO

- ☑ Ask children what they are learning and thinking about.

- ☑ Document what children are exploring by taking photos, hanging up their work (e.g., pictures, writing), and preparing posters that show the story of their explorations and discoveries.

- ☑ Place documentation of children's work and thinking in learning centers so that children and parents can reflect on what is going on in different areas of the room.

DON'T Ignore children's work.

23. Encourage children to contribute to group discussions.

DO

- ☑ Allow children to contribute during circle time and other discussion times. Remind them of the appropriate classroom rule (e.g., raise your hand or wait till the other person is done talking).

- ☑ Ask individual children to contribute to discussions. Especially for hesitant and shy children, start with questions that have no right or wrong answer ("What did you think about the story?").

DON'T Force children to participate.

24. Encourage conversation between children.

DO

- ☑ With several children, bring up subjects of common interest like the activity they are doing, common likes, other commonalities (e.g., "Both Suzy and Johnny have a dog.").

- ☑ Start a conversation then allow and encourage children to continue it.

DON'T Dominate children's conversations, but prompt and support children to respond to one another.

25. Encourage children to use their language for expressing feelings, ideas, and needs.

DO

- ☑ Ask children what they are feeling or thinking about.

- ☑ Support children to tell each other how different events make them feel, such as, "I'm angry when you take my toy car."

- ☑ Encourage children to tell each other and adults what they want, such as, "I want you to give me a turn."

- ☑ Accept children's descriptions of how they are feeling.

DON'T Tell a child how to feel or how not to feel.

Preschool Years

26. Read to children.

DO

- ☑ Introduce children to all types of books, including storybooks, concept books, wordless books, and dictionaries.

- ☑ Read favorite stories over and over again.

- ☑ Provide opportunities and materials for children to reenact stories with flannel boards, props, puppets.

- ☑ Read stories that reflect the cultural traditions of the children.

- ☑ Read to children throughout the day individually, in pairs, and as a group.

DON'T Limit reading to large group time.

27. Participate in discussions with children about books.

DO

☑ Ask children to predict what a story will be about from the title or pictures or guess what will happen next.

☑ Ask children what they liked or disliked about a story.

☑ Ask questions that relate stories to daily experiences (e.g., "In the story, Alex went swimming. Do you go swimming?").

☑ Ask factual questions about stories and questions about the pictures (e.g., "Was it summer or winter in the story? How could you tell?").

DON'T Discourage a child's excitement about reading by constantly demanding that he or she answer questions.

28. Encourage children to read.

DO

☑ Encourage children to help read story titles and other easy phrases.

☑ Encourage children to read their own and others' names, labels of common objects in the room, and labels of activity areas.

☑ Place advertisements, food boxes, and can labels in a play kitchen for children to read.

☑ Label art supplies and things in the science area.

☑ Encourage children to write and read their own stories.

DON'T Limit the availability of books, pictures, and magazines.

Preschool Years

29. Set up a writing center.

DO

- ☑ Identify an area of the room as a writing center.

- ☑ Include materials such as paper, pencils, markers, chalk, chalkboards, notebooks, typewriters, computers, and staplers.

- ☑ Prepare a journal for each child and encourage him or her to put entries in the journal (e.g., words, marks, pictures).

- ☑ Have children share the work they are doing in the writing center with each other.

DON'T Make work in the writing center mandatory or adult directed.

30. Provide opportunities for children to copy names, letters, and other meaningful words.

DO

- ☑ Write children's names slowly on their papers, saying each individual letter as it is written.

- ☑ Write children's names on a separate piece of paper for them to copy the name to their own paper.

- ☑ Provide opportunities for children to write their names on art projects, class charts, and so on.

DON'T Expect children to learn to form letters without good models.

31. Provide a variety of "play spaces" so that children can select from a number of different play options.

DO

☑ Set up a variety of play areas such as writing center, book area, art, dramatic play, blocks, sensory play (e.g., sand and water), and manipulatives.

☑ Include a variety of different objects and materials in each play area to support a variety of different types of play.

DON'T Expect all children to engage in the same types of play.

32. Play games that include physical activities with children.

DO

☑ Play games and sing songs that encourage action, such as "Ring around the Rosy," "Duck, Duck, Goose," "Mother (Captain) May I?" "Musical Chairs," and "Simon Says."

☑ Play in appropriate areas, outside or inside, in a space large enough for the game.

DON'T Control children's physical activities.

33. **Provide social opportunities to meet and play with other children and adults.**

DO

☑ Allow time in the day for free play.

☑ Include parents and other family members on field trips.

☑ Have parties or special days (e.g., day at the park) with other classes.

☑ Invite community members to share their interests and skills with the children, for example, invite a builder to come and share some blueprints with a group of children who have created structures in the block area.

DON'T Discourage parents from taking an active role in program activities.

34. **Show interest and enjoyment in children by listening to music, playing games, or dancing with them.**

DO

☑ Interact with children as they play. Show interest in their actions by asking open-ended questions or reflecting their comments (e.g., "That cake looks good. What's in it?" "You're making that elephant walk up the hill. What will the elephant do now?").

☑ Move through all the different play areas, commenting on the different activities in which children are engaged.

☑ Help children share their play activities with each other during a circle or meeting time.

☑ During gross motor and music times, sing, dance, and run (when appropriate) with children. Play ball or other games with children, not directing the activity but only participating.

DON'T Ignore what children are doing.

35. Include a variety of materials in each play area so that children with differing abilities and interests can play together.

DO

☑ Examine the materials included in each play area from the perspective of each child in the room.

☑ Adapt any materials to assure that a child with a disability or challenge can participate in the play area.

☑ Talk to children about the play areas and the materials they would like to find there.

DON'T Expect children to conform to adult expectations of how a particular play area should be used.

36. Observe and record what children are doing during play.

DO

☑ Spend time in each play area.

☑ Record what children are doing and saying during their play.

☑ Display artifacts and pictures of what children accomplished during their play.

☑ Share with parents how children are playing and what it means about their development.

☑ Use the information gathered by watching children's play to develop new play areas or enrich existing areas.

DON'T Interrupt children's play.

Preschool Years

37. Provide children with at least 35 to 40 minutes of uninterrupted, child-directed, free choice time daily.

DO

☑ Set up a rich play environment so that children can engage in play for at least 35 to 40 minutes without reaching the limits of the materials or play options.

☑ Observe what is happening as children play so that you can expand and enrich the play by adding materials, suggesting an additional story line, or asking a thought-provoking question.

☑ Protect children's play from interruption.

DON'T Dominate children's play.

38. Encourage children to participate in simple group problem-solving situations.

DO

☑ Allow children to vote for group activities.

☑ Allow children to suggest activities and use their suggestions.

DON'T Make all decisions for children.

39. Encourage expression of feelings that are of a more abstract nature.

DO

☑ Help children identify their feelings (e.g., "You feel sad" or "You miss your mom.").

☑ Talk about the feelings of characters in books.

☑ Ask and encourage children to tell how they feel.

☑ Allow verbal expression of all feelings.

DON'T Disregard or minimize children's feelings.

40. Use guidance techniques such as modeling and encouraging expected behavior to help development of self-control in children.

DO

☑ Tell children what to do instead of what not to do.

☑ When a child has a problem, talk through possible solutions. Ask what can be done or make suggestions and help the child decide whether the suggestion will work.

☑ Demonstrate appropriate behavior.

☑ Encourage children to use words instead of physical action to respond to problems. Model talking the way you expect children to speak.

DON'T Expect children to anticipate necessary behaviors without providing cues or prompts.

41. Provide affection and support, comforting children if they cry and reassuring them if they are fearful.

DO

☑ Talk matter-of-factly to children (e.g., "You fell down and hurt your knee, but we're going to get an ice pack and that will help you.").

☑ Reflect children's feelings (e.g., "You're sad right now.").

☑ Allow the child to indicate whether he or she wishes to be held, hugged, or picked up, or ask, "Would you like to sit on my lap for a while?"

☑ Help the child to move on to a different activity (e.g., "Would you like to go to the sandbox? I will go with you.")

DON'T Minimize feelings that children express.

Preschool Years

42. Offer experiences to alleviate children's fears.

DO

☑ Read stories about common fears and talk about them.

☑ Allow and encourage children to talk openly about their fears. Reflect their feelings (e.g., "You don't like the dark.").

DON'T Belittle or demean children's fears.

43. Structure activities that require sharing.

DO

☑ Provide enough toys or supplies (e.g., blocks) for several children to play at once.

☑ Provide a variety of toys (e.g., large and small blocks of various shapes).

☑ Choose supplies so that there are enough for each child to have something but so that each child has different things. For example, when making cookies with five children, have two spoons, one bowl, and several measuring cups. Encourage sharing and turn taking with materials.

☑ Help children to pass food to one another during snack, rather than the teacher serving everyone.

☑ Play games that require sharing materials, like passing a ball.

DON'T Restrict activities that would provide opportunities for children to engage in turn taking, requesting objects, and waiting.

44. Encourage children to participate in simple group problem-solving situations.

DO

☑ Allow children to vote for group activities.

☑ Allow children to suggest activities and use their suggestions

DON'T Make all decisions for children.

45. Spend one-on-one time with each child each day.

DO

☑ Ask a question about some unique aspect of the child's life, such as a recent trip to Grandma's house.

☑ Comment on a specific activity you observed the child doing.

☑ Share a book or object in which this child will be uniquely interested.

DON'T Ask all children the same questions.

For additional information on appraising quality child care, visit our Web site at http://www.earlychilded.delmar.com

Preschool Years

Appendix A

Resources for Exploring Cultural Diversity

Resources for Understanding Cultural Diversity and Creating Culturally Sensitive Early Childhood Environments

Cultural competence is the willingness and ability to value the importance of culture. It is a perspective that values differences and is responsive to diversity in lifestyle. Cultural competence is developmental, community focused, and family oriented. It is a way of interacting with children and families that communicates a valuing of differences and integration of cultural attitudes and beliefs into all aspects of a program, including books, toys, pictures, and notices. Culturally sensitive programs provide opportunities for staff and families to explore personal beliefs and biases and to incorporate family traditions into program activities. The following resources can support an understanding and development of culturally sensitive programs.

The authors and Delmar Learning make every effort to ensure that all Internet resources are accurate at the time of printing. However, due to the fluid, time-sensitive nature of the Internet, we cannot guarantee that all URLs and Web site addresses will remain current for the duration of this edition.

Web Sites

Teaching Tolerance
http://www.tolerance.org

This site, sponsored by the Southern Poverty Law Center, provides "101 Tools for Tolerance: Simple Ideas for Promoting Equity and Celebrating Diversity." In addition, it provides links to a site for children titled Planet Tolerance.

C*L*A*S Institute
http://www.clas.uiuc.edu

This site, providing "culturally and linguistically appropriate resources," is a clearinghouse of the Early Childhood Research Institute for materials for working with different cultural groups.

Multicultural Pavilion
http://www.edchange.org/multicultural/

This multicultural Web site mainly supplies information to teachers that will assist in enhancing multicultural awareness in their classrooms. The site contains activities, resources, teaching tools, and even discussion bulletin boards where teachers can exchange ideas. There are also links to other multicultural Internet sites.

Books for Educators

de Melendez, Wilma Robles & Osterag, Vesna (1997). *Teaching young children in multicultural classrooms.* Clifton Park, NY: Delmar Learning.

    Ordering information: Delmar Learning
    5 Maxwell Drive
    Clifton Park, NY 12065
    http://www.earlychilded.delmar.com
    1-800-347-7707
    ISBN: 0-8273-7275-2

Derman-Sparks, Louise (1989). *Anti-bias curriculum: Tools for empowering young children.* Washington, DC: National Association for the Education of Young Children.

    Ordering Information: National Association for the Education
    of Young Children
    1834 Connecticut Ave. N.W.
    Washington, DC 20009-5786
    1-800-424-2460
    ISBN: 0-935989-20-X

Klein, Diane M. & Chen, Deborah (2001). *Working with children from culturally diverse backgrounds.* Clifton Park, NY: Delmar Learning.

    Ordering information: Delmar Learning
    5 Maxwell Drive
    Clifton Park, NY 12065
    http://www.earlychilded.delmar.com
    1-800-347-7707
    ISBN: 0-7668-2406-3

Paley, V. G. (1995). *Kwanzaa and me: A teacher's story.* Cambridge, MA: Harvard University Press.

Ordering information: Harvard University Press
79 Garden Street
Cambridge, MA 02138
1-800-405-1619
ISBN: 0-674-50585-9

Saderman, Nadia (1999). *Creative resources for the anti-bias classroom.* Clifton Park, NY: Delmar Learning.

Ordering information: Delmar Learning
5 Maxwell Drive
Clifton Park, NY 12065
http://www.earlychilded.delmar.com
1-800-347-7707
ISBN: 0-8273-8015-1

Wolpert, Ellen (1999). *Start seeing diversity: The basic guide to an anti-bias classroom.* St. Paul, MN.

Ordering information: Gryphon House
P.O. Box 207
Beltsville, MD 20704-0207
1-800-638-0928
ISBN: 1-884834-77-9

Sample Room Arrangements

Infant Environment

Angela Capone

 There are a variety of ways to set up the physical environment for quality infant care. The room arrangement shown in Figure A–1 is simply one environmental design. However, there are key characteristics and considerations that should be evident in physical setup of all infant environments. The primary goal is to design an environment that enables caregivers to provide consistent responsiveness to each infant's expression of need. In addition, the environment should reflect the unique characteristics of infancy. Here are some of the factors we considered when designing our infant space.

Safety Is of Utmost Importance

It goes without saying that infant spaces must be safe havens: electrical outlets must be covered, cords must be covered and out of reach, toys and furniture must be in good working order and free from rough edges, and objects that infants might use to pull themselves up must be stable. We suggest you review your state's licensing regulations to assure your space is free of hidden hazards.

Babies Need Space for Movement

Jean Piaget described infancy as the sensorimotor period of development. During this stage of development, babies coordinate information gathered through their senses and movement to develop a physical understanding of the world. It is logical, therefore, that babies need room to move. Since babies develop at differing rates, the environment needs to have space for mobile babies to move safely about, as well as space for less mobile infants to be protected. When thinking of space for movement, consider ways to help infants truly explore how their bodies move. For example, have low mattresses for infants to climb onto, soft pillows for infants to climb over, and safe, sturdy "bars" for infants to pull themselves up with. Infants who roll will need space to roll about, protected from mobile infants who are not yet able to maneuver around babies or objects in their way. While it may be tempting to place babies in "bouncy" seats for safety sake, these seats do not allow them to freely explore how their bodies move and, oftentimes, can inhibit exploration of objects and interactions with adults and other infants. A more effective way of allowing infants to move freely about and protect less mobile infants is to set up some soft barriers and sit on the floor with the infants.

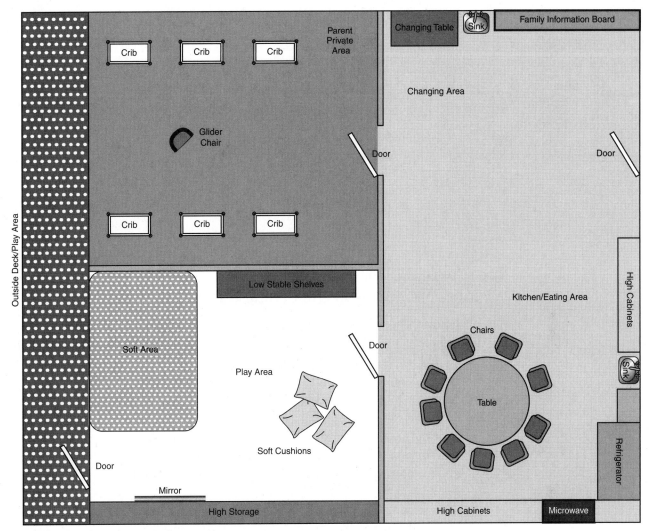

FIGURE A–1 Sample infant classroom. (Courtesy of Angela Capone.)

Sensory Stimulation In the Environment

Since, as Piaget says, babies learn through their senses, it is important to think about types and amounts of sensory stimulation in the environment. You will want to consider the sights, sounds, and smells. The environment should provide a variety of stimulation, taking care not to overwhelm the infant. Think about the light in the room, what type of music you play at different times of the day, and about introducing different scents. When placing pictures in the environment, consider the fact that much of an infant's exploration takes place at a height of 20–25 inches above the floor, and even lower when infants are lying down or crawling. Perhaps you could carefully place some family pictures on the floor and cover them with contact paper for safety. Consider the following:

- Incandescent lamps provide a softer, more natural light source than fluorescent lights.
- Vary the floor covering, use tile in areas for wet play or eating, carpet in play areas, soft blankets over the carpeting in some other areas of the room.
- Open windows to bring the outdoor smells indoors and let a breeze blow gently, perhaps across a wind chime that responds with a delightful sound.

The Physical Environment Must Accommodate a Variety of Feeding and Sleeping Schedules

One of the ways infants express their uniqueness is in their feeding, sleeping, and playing schedules. Each infant establishes a schedule based on his or her own temperament, natural rhythms, and needs. Even in group care, infants should not be expected to fit an arbitrary schedule. In order to accommodate their differences, the physical space must be designed with separate areas for sleeping, caregiving routines such as feeding and diapering, and active play. Pay close attention to ways in which the design supports, or inhibits, a caregiver's ability to oversee the entire room while interacting with an individual child.

The Physical Space Should Reflect the Size and Perspective of the Infant

When designing the physical space, consider the infant's point of view. Younger babies will have a greater sense of comfort and security in smaller spaces. Larger spaces typically lend themselves to more infants, more noise, and, potentially, more chaos. Think about arranging the room with smaller areas to create a sense of enclosure.

The Environment Should Provide for Adult Comfort

When designing the physical environment, it is important to consider the comfort of the adults who care for infants. Have a comfortable area, perhaps including a couch, rocking chair, cushions, and big pillows. This area should be a place where an adult can relax and have a nurturing, one-to-one interaction with an infant.

Provide a Space for Private Parent Interaction

Parents will often want to visit with their infant during the day. Some may come to nurse or feed their child, and others to play or rock their child to sleep. Consider the room arrangement from a parent's point of view. Is there a comfortable place to be with their child? Does the space provide privacy? Is the space a pleasant place?

Storage Space Should Be Easily Accessible

Storage is an important element of environmental design. Although there will be many large items that must be stored in a hall closet or room outside the infant care area, storage in the room should be sufficient and strategically placed so that caregivers have easy access to necessary items without leaving infants unsupervised. For example, items necessary for caregiving routines should be readily accessible in each area. This enables the caregiver to maintain an ongoing interaction with an infant during diapering, for example, while having items such as diapers and wipes within arm's reach. Toys and other play materials that infants can use independently should be stored on safe, sturdy, low shelves or in baskets. Toys and other materials that are meant for adults should be stored in high cabinets. Storage is also important to maintain an environment that is free from clutter. More is not always better; using just a few well-chosen play objects and books can entice an infant into greater exploration.

Outdoor Environments Are As Important As Indoor Environments

It is important for infants to have time outdoors as well as indoors. Sometimes that time will be spent in a stroller, sometimes in a park. It is also important to consider a space just outside the classroom where infants can feel the breeze, smell the flowers, watch the clouds, and see the sunlight. This outdoor environment, which is full of naturally occurring sensory experiences, is a great place to read with an infant, talk about all that is going on, and play with favorite objects. Designing this outdoor space will take the same level of consideration as planning the indoor environment: Are infants protected from the direct sunlight? Is the area free of hazards? Is there a soft area for infants on which they can crawl? Is the area comfortable for adults? Are play materials easily accessible? Can mobile infants move freely and easily about while less mobile infants remain safe?

While this is not an exhaustive description of how to set up an infant environment, it should provide some critical ideas for consideration. As you read through the Infancy section of *Childmate,* you will find more information on each of these recommendations, as well as some other ideas for designing your space. Remember, well-designed infant environments take into account all the things that make infancy a unique period of development. A well-thought-out design can protect infants from requiring a barrage of "no's" and meet their needs for emotional security.

Two-Year-Old Environment

Irene J. Dowdle

The room arrangement shown in Figure A–2 was designed to welcome both the children and their parents. It is also a room that makes interacting with the children a pleasure for the teachers. This room was designed for 10 children and three teachers.

An adult entering this classroom will be able to see every activity area in the room. All the shelves, with the exception of the cubbies, are low enough for an adult to see over. A child entering this room will see a large open area and lots of hidden areas just waiting to be explored. This two-year-old classroom has the same activity areas found in an environment for older preschoolers but with fewer choices and more duplication of toys.

As you enter the room, you will see the cubbies located to the right. The cubbies are 4 feet tall. Located inside each cubbie are hooks for coats, hats, and other items to be hung up. Boots, shoes, and comfort things from home can be placed on one of the two lower shelves. Each cubbie is identified with the child's photo and name. This allows for the emerging independence of a two-year-old. Above each cubbie is a space for teachers to put information for the parents, which is to be sent home. This space also has a hook for parents to hang pocketbooks and things while they assist their child in getting ready for the day. Locked cabinets are located above this space. At the end of the cubbies, just as you walk in the door, is an open closet for hanging coats. These hooks are at an adult's height. Hopefully this will encourage those parents who have time to take their coats off and stay for a while. There is a low, carpeted, open bench located in front of the cubbies. This bench is helpful for putting on and taking off boots and shoes. It is also an object that children can crawl under or over or lie on. The back of the low shelf for the blocks, which faces the cubbie area, is a great place to display the children's handiwork.

The next area is the construction and building activity area. By providing a limited amount of material, which nonetheless varies in size, shape, and texture, the children can create all sorts of things (*NC Guide for the Early Years,* 1997). As the children play with these materials, they will develop their cognitive, perceptual, and motor abilities. One open shelf contains various blocks, while the open shelf opposite will contain different toys to incorporate into the children's play. For example, there may be people and dinosaurs, which may later be changed to cars and trucks. As the children grow and develop throughout the year, a wider variety of items may be placed on these open shelves. This area also has a table for building on. This will make all the blocks accessible to children who use a wheelchair or special stroller. There are wedges that can also be used if a child cannot sit independently yet wants to play on the floor

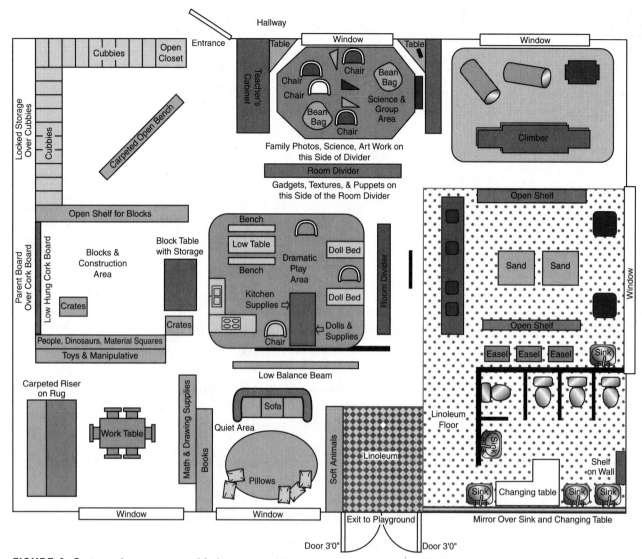

FIGURE A–2 Sample two-year-old classroom. (Courtesy of Irene J. Dowdle.)

beside another child. Crates and cardboard boxes can also be found in this area. It should be noted that some of these construction items might be taken into other areas of the classroom as the children incorporate them into their play. An example of this would be a child taking the tool belt into the dramatic play area to "fix" the sink.

A low-hung bulletin board with the parent information board hung above it is found in the construction area. The bulletin board will have a variety of artwork and photos on it. Having the parent information board above it encourages parents to view their child's artwork and photos of their children at play during the day.

Moving on around the room, you come to the toy and manipulative activity area. There is a child-size table, two open shelves, and a soft rug with a low foam bench on it. One low shelf holds large pieces of paper and crayons for scribbling. The teachers make the choices of what will be on the open shelves, but the children also make their own choice. They are allowed to choose what they want to play with and in what way. Manipulative play helps children to test their emerging problem-solving skills and improves their fine motor skills. Some items that may be put on the shelves are puzzles, large wooden beads for stringing, and nesting toys. Children are encouraged to engage in parallel play through the provision of duplicate toys and materials. This area may also be used in other ways. A child may decide to bring a baby doll from the dramatic play area and put the baby to bed on the foam platform located on the rug. This area has a large window that is low enough for the children to view the outside world. This window and the window in the quiet area are great places to display plants that have been grown from seed as part of a science project.

The book area is next. This area is designed to be quieter than the other activity areas. There is a sofa, and several pillows are spread out on the floor, on a soft, pale blue rug. The books are displayed in such a way that the children can easily see and reach each one. The open shelf opposite the books holds a few soft, stuffed animals. The sofa faces the window and helps to give this area an enclosed feeling. Teachers can see over the sofa and shelves, but the children will feel they are in an isolated area. Children can take the books and other items out of this area to be shared elsewhere in the room. Books and reading should not be confined to one location.

As you continue on, you come to the double glass doors that lead to the outside play areas. These doors, along with the large windows, provide a great deal of natural light inside the classroom. They also allow the children to enjoy the outside world while they are inside. Bird feeders and birdhouses placed within view of these windows and doors will encourage the children to ask questions about the world around them. The floor in this area is linoleum, which makes for easy cleanup if the children come in from playing with wet or dirty shoes.

The bathroom is located to the right of the doors leading to the outside play area. This location allows for easy access to bathrooms when outside. There are three regular child-size toilets plus another child-size toilet with support bars on each side. There are three child-size sinks to decrease time waiting in line to wash hands and brush teeth. There is an adult sink and a changing table. (Many children in a two-year-old classroom will be at various stages of potty training.) There is a long mirror placed over the sinks and changing table that allows the children to view themselves when at the sink. If this room is used for full-time child care, the sleeping cots can be stored in this area near the double doors leading outside.

The sensory play area is next. This area includes activities such as water play, sand play, and painting. There are three easels set side-by-side, which allows the children to observe each other. The floor in this area is tile, with a covered drain for easy cleanup. There is a child-size sink for cleaning hands before moving on to other areas. The extra large window allows for viewing the outside as well as providing plenty of natural light. There is a "clothesline" with clips under the window for hanging art to dry. There are two sand tables, which provide play space for at least six children. The materials for the sand tables as well as the various art supplies are chosen by the teacher and placed on the open shelves for the children to select. Also in this area is a long, low table with a shelf underneath. The shelf holds the water buckets and supplies for water play. Providing several buckets at one time allows for several children to play side-by-side, which is a characteristic of this age group. This table can also be used for other art activities such as finger painting, using play dough, and bathing baby dolls.

Beside the sensory area is the gross motor area. This area is for large muscle experiences, emotional outlets, and exercise, which are essential to all aspects of development. Climbing a climber also provides children with a wonderful opportunity to gain a different perspective on their environment. Children learn and develop, which helps to build self-esteem. There are two tunnels for crawling through and a rocking boat that can be turned over to make steps. The window in this area looks out into the hallway, giving the children views of other activities and people. The low cabinet has a mirror for children to view themselves at play.

Located near the entrance and near the gross motor area is the science and group area. The low cabinet has a felt board attached, which is used during a short group time. There is a rug placed over the room's carpet, and seating of various types is provided. Foam wedges and beanbags are provided for children both with and without physical disabilities. This area has two corner tables. One holds a fish aquarium, which the children can take turns feeding each day during group time. The other table can be used for various items relating to the children's interest. The class can have an ant farm, raise butterflies, or watch the habits of a live animal. The teacher's cabinet is locked and provides a work surface and also storage for science books, felt story supplies, and records. This area should have a tape or CD player for stories, music, and movement. The room divider that separates this area from the rest of the room provides a great place to put family pictures, animal pictures, and various photos related to daily activities. The back of this low room divider has pegs, which hold puppets. The children will hopefully discover that this is a great place for puppet shows. It also has items similar to what are found in a child's "busy box." Everyday items can be attached to this room divider to provide the children with hours of interest. Such items as an old-fashioned doorbell, windup alarm clock, locks, shoes with laces, large snaps, large buttons, and pinwheels will help to keep their young minds busy.

The last activity area is the dramatic play area, located in the center of the room. Two-year-olds are just beginning to play simple make-believe games. A large rug defines this area. The props are few. There is an L-shaped cooking center, which has a stove, oven, refrigerator, and sink. One side of the open shelf holds plates, cups, and cooking items, along with play food. All these items are few in number to limit confusion. There are also a picnic-style table, two large doll beds, dolls representing different races, and doll supplies. Again, because of the young age of these children, choices are limited and items are changed as the children and teachers see the need. The room divider that faces the sensory area has a mirror on one end and pegs with a variety of dress-up clothes on the other end. The other side holds children's artwork. There is a low balance beam near this area. Children at this age are beginning to try out new skills, and this provides one such opportunity. It is a tool for their imagination. The beam can be a train, a horse, or a building platform. I placed the dramatic play area in the center of the room because I feel this area will become a part of all the other areas, and vice versa.

Two-year-olds are developing at a very fast rate in all the developmental domains. This classroom is child centered and includes age-appropriate physical, temporal, and interpersonal environments.

Figures A–3 and A–4 show other sample room arrangements for a two-year-old classroom.

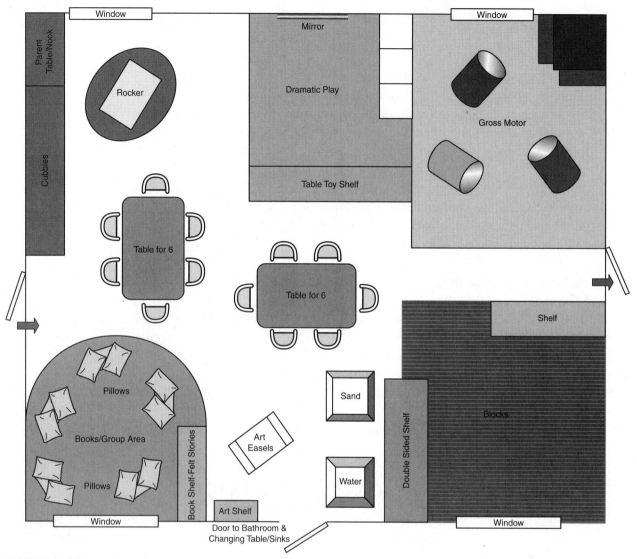

FIGURE A–3 Sample two-year-old classroom. (Courtesy of Nancy R. Holland.)

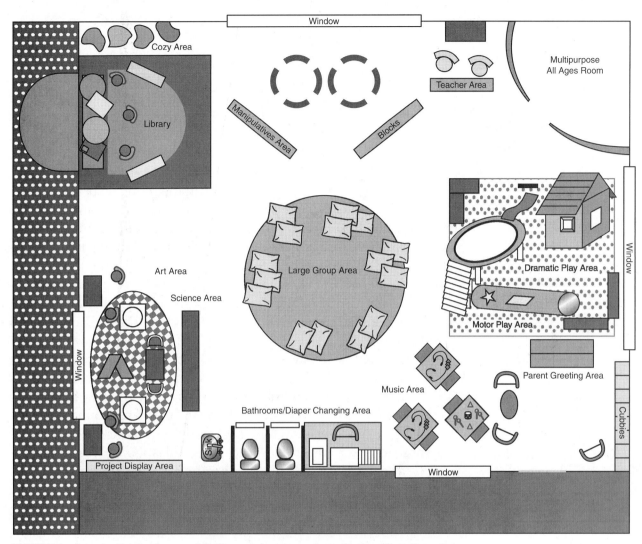

FIGURE A–4 Sample two-year-old classroom. (Courtesy of Jeannie Wilson.)

Three-Year-Old Classroom

Jeannie Wilson

 When designing this three-year-old classroom (Figure A–5), I first tried to make it a place where children feel like they belong. This sense of belonging can help build a child's self-esteem. I did this by making it an aesthetically appealing place with colorful walls and furnishings and designing it with the children's needs in mind. The colors of the room are cool to help create a cool, calm feeling in the room. Also, a light color is used on the walls to make the space expand and the room look large. This keeps children from feeling closed in and confined. Windows and skylights are used throughout the room to allow children to look outside and also to allow natural light to come in. This reduces the dependency on fluorescent lighting and avoids any adverse effects of artificial lighting. Plants are used throughout the room to enhance the flow of light and provide a glimpse of nature. The room design allows for children to work competently and independently by providing a wide variety of materials, space to work in, and easy access to those materials. This sense of independence and self-management is important in promoting positive self-esteem in children. Areas of the room are divided by boundaries to inform the child where the activities are to take place. Boundaries such as bookcases, balance beams, and shelves define where the area begins and ends. In the arrangement of learning areas, quiet areas are separated from noisy areas and messy areas are kept together in a location with easy cleanup. I tried to arrange furniture in a way that would allow children to participate in group play or solitary play, both of which are important experiences. An attempt was made to include developmentally appropriate activities in the classroom so that typical three-year-old skills could be developed and practiced. Three-year-olds are beginning to take turns, play cooperatively with others, play in groups, and dramatize play. They also can listen in order to learn, alternate feet in stair climbing, wash hands unassisted, and exercise lively imaginations.

A spare room is located toward the upper left-hand corner of the room. This multipurpose room can be used for a teacher who wants to conduct small group activities. It can also be made available to the two-year-olds, four-year-olds, and five-year-olds so that larger, multiage groups can work together. The doorway into the three-year-olds' classroom has an observation window. This window placement allows parents and children to see the activity of the classroom before entering. A shy or hesitant child can become familiar with what is going on inside before entering the classroom, which eases the transition. As you enter the room, the children's cubbies are located on the left-hand side. Directly in front of the doorway is a wall containing pictures of the children and their families. This display can help draw the children into the room and make them feel at home. On the right-hand side of the

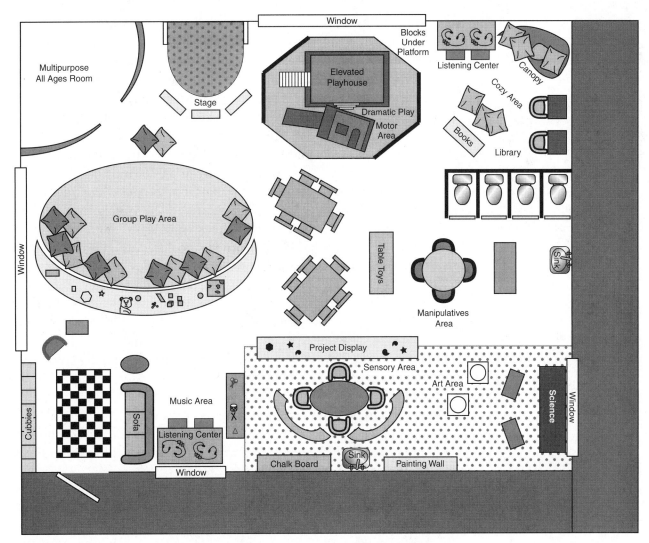

FIGURE A–5 Sample three-year-old classroom. (Courtesy of Jeannie Wilson.)

doorway is a parent greeting area. This location contains a couch and chair, as well as a parent information board. Parents can sit with their children on arrival in the morning to make sure the children feel comfortable in their environment. This area is stocked with books from the library, so books to allow for parent-child reading time are on hand. Parents can also use this area to spend time with their children upon pickup or observe their child at play. Informal teacher-parent meetings can also take place in this area.

To the right of the doorway is the music area. Music of all kinds encourages self-expression and permits a variety of movement and feelings to be shown openly and freely. The music center includes a pegboard on which are hung instruments, scarves, and ribbons to accompany and move to the music with. Also included in the music area is a listening station that enhances auditory awareness. This allows children to work on listening skills and enjoy music as a solitary task or with a friend. By learning songs and music games, children can improve their perceptual-motor development.

The pegboard located in the music center divides that area from the art and science areas. The art area is located near the science area to encourage shared knowledge between the two. For example, activities such as color mixing, using clay with water, and mixing tempera paints relate to scientific principles. On the wall next to the science area are areas for art activities. This area takes advantage of unused wall space. More toward the left is a wall area that acts as a chalkboard for the children's artwork. As you go toward the right, the wall is covered with protective coating or paneling that allows children to paint directly on the walls or hang materials to be painted or colored upon. Finger painting and painting on broad surfaces with large brushes encourages a freedom of movement that permits children to express themselves more fully. These wall artwork areas allow children to work side-by-side in creating art. In between these two areas of the wall is a sink for easy preparation of material and cleanup. This area also includes a table at which projects can be carried out. Several chairs are provided, promoting the sharing of materials and artistic ideas. Shelving provides art materials that the children can easily access. Materials such as crayons, pens, scissors, and hole punches help to develop children's fine motor skills. Also, material such as clay or play dough can be useful in letting children ventilate feeling by pounding and poking. Open-ended materials, such as those listed here, help stimulate creativity in children.

The art activities area is divided from the quiet areas by a project shelf. Artwork and projects can be displayed on this shelf to give the children pride in their work. The floor in the entire area (including the art, science, and sensory areas) is covered by tile. The tile is textured to prevent falls from spills, durable, and easy to clean. The sensory tables are located in this area and are arranged to allow several children to play at once, which encourages cooperative play. The location of the sensory tables next to the science area allows for experimentation and exchange between the two centers. The science center includes a window housing plants and experiments carried out by the children. The location of a window here provides a view of the changing seasons, outdoor scenes, and a variety of sights that can be a focus for conversation or learning activities in science. A table provides an area for these experiments to take place.

The next area, as you continue counterclockwise around the room, is the manipulative/table toys area. Two tables are provided for playing with tabletop toys and puzzles. These toys are located on a nearby shelf. A manipulatives table is also present in this area. This table has a table-top for use with interlocking blocks and other manipulative toys. Found objects and unique toys are provided in this area because exposure to different kinds of objects can help children develop classification skills and teach them to have different responses to different objects. This area allows children to develop and practice fine motor skills. The tables and chairs are arranged in this area so children get the message that they can work together or participate in parallel play.

As you continue counterclockwise around the room, the bathroom is next. Several child-size toilets are provided so that several children can use the facility at the same time. The bathroom is located near the children's cubbies so that supplies and extra clothes can be located easily. The bathroom is also located in close proximity to the door leading to the outside playground. This location allows for easy access from outside. Also located next to the doorway are child-size sinks to promote proper hygiene for the children.

In the upper right-hand corner of the room is the library area. Posted on the walls of this area are clippings of people and photographs of children displaying different emotions and feelings. This provides opportunities for teachers and children to discuss feelings and increase the children's ability to express their own feelings. This area contains a shelf with books and puppets as well as child-size rocking chairs and pillows for the children. The library is located close to the parent greeting area so that parents can interact with their children through books. A listening area is provided in this area to allow children to listen to recorded stories and enhance their auditory awareness. In the corner of the room is a canopy extending out from the wall. This area acts like a tent to provide children with a quiet place to go. These types of spaces are important so children can relax and recharge during the daily routine of group living. A large window in this area allows for observation from the hallway into the classroom, or the other way around.

Along the center of the upper wall is the physical/gross motor play area. The flooring in this area is padded to ensure safety in the case of falls. The area includes stairs that lead to a doorway on a slightly elevated platform. Doors, gates, and pass-throughs can be incorporated into indoor play areas to help children experiment with the concepts of inside and outside and enhance imaginative play. This platform is also accessible by a ramp. This area can be incorporated into the dramatic play area to simulate a house or building. Soft climbing mats lead to a more elevated play area that can also be accessed via a ladder from the other side. A ladder offers motor challenges and requires the child to concentrate when getting on or off the platform. By providing multiple means of entry, crowding and confrontations on the platform are reduced. This play area is elevated off the floor high enough to allow children to play either above or underneath. A window is located at the top of the elevated structure so children can see outside the classroom from a different perspective. Mirrors are located adjacent to the climbing areas around the platform so children can see their gross motor actions and increase their visual awareness. Underneath the play loft is the block area, which also contains toy animals and cars for imaginative play. This area requires teachers to get on the level of the children in play and enhances the interactive learning experience. Balance beam divisions surround several sides of this physical/gross motor area. This allows the children to test their skills in balancing, gross motor skills, and perceptual-motor skills. These skills can also be practiced on stairs and ladders in the area. The balance beam divides this area from the others, cutting down on running and distinguishing where physical activities should take place. The balance beam may also help contain blocks and other toys within the area and reduce messes.

Located on the wall behind the play structure is a window allowing children to see into the four-year-olds' classroom. This can be used for entertainment and to allow children to develop a familiarity with the classroom that they will later move to. There is also another observation window on the left-hand side of the room that allows children to see into the two-year-old class, which they just left. This opportunity to see their old friends at play may make it easier to transition.

As you continue counterclockwise around the room, the next area is the dramatic play area. This area includes a stage for skits, puppet shows, or class presentations. The back of the stage is lined with mirrors, and mirrors are also located in front of the stage. This allows children to watch their actions as they play and explore their body movements. Next to the stage is a pegboard on which children can hang dress-up clothing. There is also a shelf for other props, puppets, and materials for use in the dramatic play area. A variety of home-life materials and props allow children to express how they see their own world of family, parents, and siblings. Dramatizations also allow children to act out many roles and help them deal with some of the demands placed on them.

Toward the center of the room is a large rug. This area has been left open so that it may be used for group time or large group activities. Pillows are also provided in this area so children can use it as an additional play area or expand an activity from another center that requires more room.

The design of this room maximizes the use of possible surfaces. Walls and floors are used in many different ways, to communicate, display, and provide activity space. This can be seen in the use of a window between classrooms to allow for communication. Walls are also used to hang mirrors that can communicate information to the children about how their bodies move. Furthermore, walls and surfaces are used to display children's artwork and pictures from home and school. The walls in the art area are used for art activities. This utilizes space that might not have been used and prevents an easel from taking up more floor space. Different types of flooring make the floor a working space. A balance of floor surfaces is necessary and can also make organization of the room easier. By providing soft flooring, tile flooring, and carpet in specific areas, the floor helps to define activity spaces. This is also true of the physical/gross motor area, which is divided from the other areas by a balance beam. This helps to define the area and acts as a partition to lessen the amount of running and traffic in the area.

Figures A–6 and A–7 show other sample room arrangements for a three-year-old classroom.

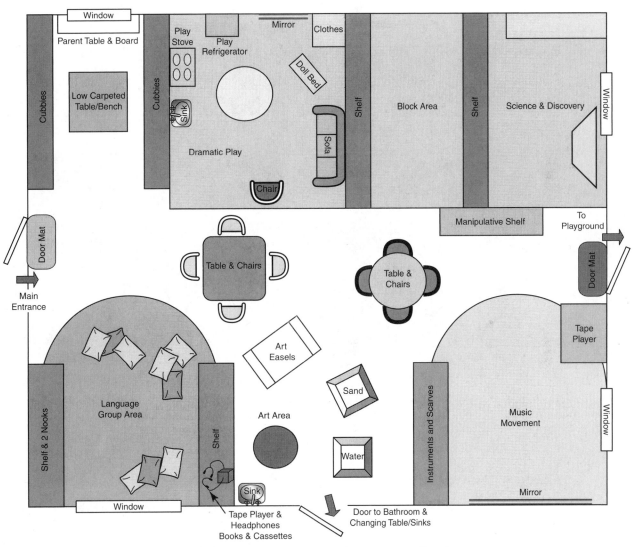

FIGURE A–6 Sample three-year-old classroom. (Courtesy of Nancy R. Holland.)

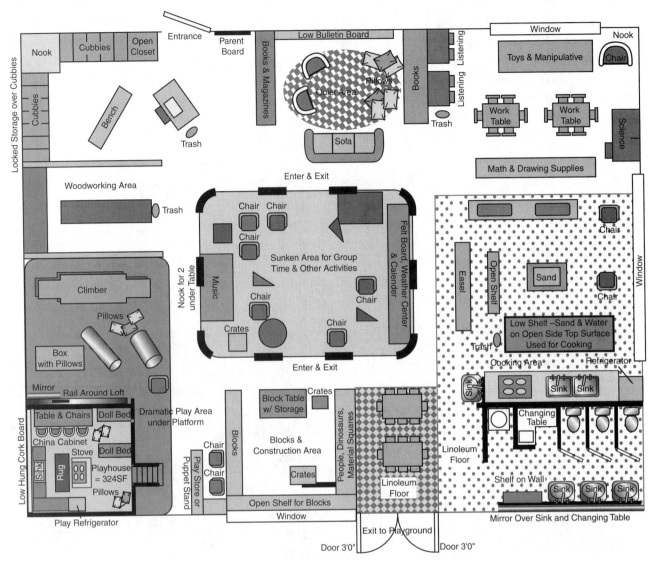

FIGURE A–7 Sample three-year-old classroom. (Courtesy of Irene J. Dowdle.)

Four-Year-Old Classroom

Nancy R. Holland

As you enter the four-year-old classroom shown in Figure A–8, if you turn to the left you will find cubbies for the children. These are labeled with each child's name and photograph. Just as each child needs a place to call his or her own, the parents also need an area in which to place their belongings. The entry area includes a table, bulletin board, and cubby shelf for the parents. Also in this entry is a low, carpeted table or bench where the child and parent can sit together on arrival and departure. I chose to group the cubbies and the language area together so it is quieter when entering the classroom

All the shelves are low and open to encourage autonomy and are used to separate the activity areas. Carpet is also used to define boundaries. There are no long, open spaces to encourage running.

The dramatic area is backed up to the one set of cubbies. Putting the cubbies back-to-back with the sink and stove help stabilize the furniture. In this area are a table, doll bed, chest of drawers (with dress-up clothes), mirror, and kitchen furniture. The kitchen utensils can hang on the back of the cubby, on pegs. They can be outlined with a solid color to promote returning items to their place. If a window is not available, false windows can be added with frames, mirrors, and curtains. Artificial plants can be used to separate a kitchen area from the living room area. Throughout the classroom all the real plants are hanging except the projects in the science area. Blocks are traced and labeled on the shelves for the block area and all the other areas.

The block area is next to the dramatic play area. Children can combine the two areas to extend their play. The shelf between the areas stores dress-up clothing that can be used in either area. This shelf also moves easily to increase or decrease each area. The carpet is the same in these two areas so they can be combined if needed. Four-year-olds really enjoy imitating the roles of their parents and are ready to extend their play. In storage are many theme units that can be rotated throughout the dramatic play area and block area. Children this age are beginning to play more intensely with plans and activities involving roles. The blocks include unit blocks as well as hollow blocks and accessories with animals, people, and vehicles. A smooth carpet makes it easier to build structures and bridges. Each item has a place and is labeled. Books also have their place in the block area, as well as photographs of bridges, construction sites, and even communities of different cultures.

The next area is the science and discovery area, which houses the equipment needed to do experiments and examine items. A lattice display board can be mounted on the shelf between this area and the block area. The lattice will be open enough to supervise the children visually yet give room to display the many nature items the children will bring

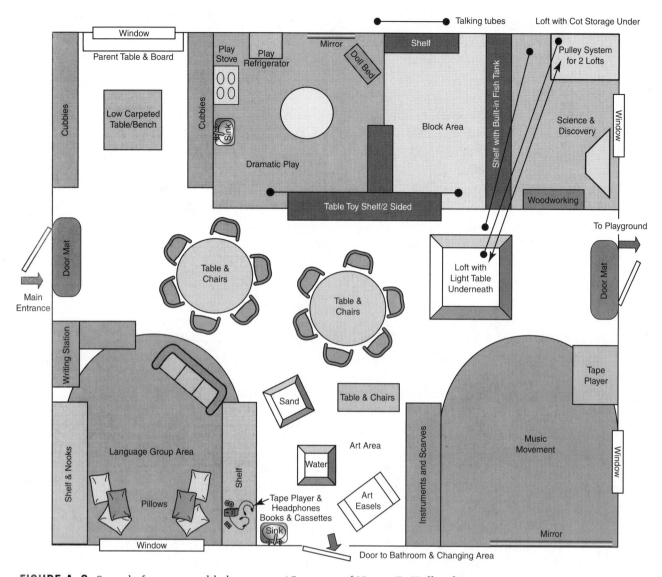

FIGURE A–8 Sample four-year-old classroom. (Courtesy of Nancy R. Holland.)

in. Also built into this dividing shelf is an aquarium, where the children can take care of fish and other creatures. There is a smaller table to encourage the children to work in small groups for short periods of time. The equipment could easily be carried to another area of the room for teacher-directed experiments. There is a window in this area to give light for the plants and experiments. Near the plants are graphing and weather charts. In the corner of the room in this science area is a storage area for the cots or mats, with doors and a small loft on top. Attached to the loft is a pulley system near the middle of the room. Also in the science area is the woodworking table, which faces into the middle of the room for easy visibility and assistance from teachers.

Across from the science area is the music and movement area. Four-year-olds still need a space to use their whole bodies. The tape player, instruments, and scarves will provide props for dancing and moving. In this area are a window and a large mirror (so the children will be able to see themselves whirling and twirling). There is also space around the mirror for photographs of the children in various dance poses and facial expressions (all about feelings).

Next to the music and movement area is the area for all the messy activities. There is an art area, where many different materials are used to paint and make collages. There are two easels and a table for a small group of children. The easels are side-by-side for associative play. Four-year-olds are becoming more creative in their art and are beginning to mold and shape objects out of clay or play dough. There is a display shelf for the creative art they now produce. Four-year-olds attend to an activity longer than before and will finish a task. There are collage materials, equipment for mixing and experimenting with colors, various types of paper, and old magazines and wallpaper books. This area is also near the sink and entrance to the bathroom. There may also be a need for the changing table if there is a child with special needs. The bathroom door is a half-door, which aids in supervision yet gives the child a feeling of a smaller, private space. Also close to the bathroom and art area are the sand and water tables. Four-year-olds are curious and are always stretching their limits. Sand and water are soothing and teach many math skills while developing fine and large muscle coordination. The children can experiment, discover, estimate, and compare. Again, many props can be stored and rotated as needed. The tables can also contain snow, grass, and other mediums to extend learning with textures.

The quietest area is next. That is the language and group area. It is located next to the main entrance. In this area there are cushions, an adult love seat, a shelf with tape player, and another shelf that is open underneath in two sections. These two sections have mats in them to create two small nooks for two children each. Nooks and crannies are important places to rest and "recharge the batteries." Since these nooks are in the language area, children can get together to read or play with felt board books. The books are clearly displayed and changed frequently. There are also books with cassettes for two children to listen to together. When this area is used for large group time, the children will be able to use the interactive bulletin board, check the calendar, read the helper chart, and participate in stories and songs. The large group area is also a good place for transitioning between games. A puppet stage can be set up in one of the available nooks.

Another area almost in the language area is the writing station. In this area there are lots of markers, crayons, pencils, and chalk. Various types and sizes of paper are available for notes and letters. The children can write letters, put them in envelopes, and even add stamps. Other props can be added as needed, such as various rubber stamps with ink pads and shaped hole punches. Other supplies include teacher-prepared paper with the children's names, alphabet, and numbers for them to copy or trace. This develops beginning writing and letter recognition. The classroom could also use the writing station as a children's sign-in station, where they can write their name as they arrive and leave or use another method of documenting their attendance. By signing themselves in and out, they become more responsible and have more ownership of the classroom. These sign-in sheets can also be used for documentation in their portfolios.

To break up the possibility of having a long running space from door to door, I have added the two main tables used for eating. These tables are also used for groups working on large puzzles or individuals working with the many manipulatives stored on the shelf that sections off the dramatic play area and block area. The manipulative shelf houses the puzzles, games, and toys that are geared toward the older three-year-olds and younger five-year-olds to give a range of skills. Four-year-olds can dress themselves more independently but need help tying shoes. Added to the table toys are objects they can tie. More toys are added that can be sorted, counted, matched, stacked, and laced. Included are smaller blocks that can be mixed and matched for more complex tabletop building.

Near the side of the room leading to the playground yet more in the middle is a 4-foot by 4-foot loft. Height is partially determined by the ceiling height and, hopefully, at least a clearance of 4 feet underneath. The purpose of the upper part of the loft is to use the pulley system connected to the smaller loft in the science area. There are various items that can be safely sent along the wire or string from one area to another. The loft can also be extended to be a ship or castle or other areas for dramatic play. The ladder to climb the two lofts also gives the four-year-olds gross motor movement practice that is otherwise hard to accomplish indoors. Other gross motor skills can be accomplished by following the leader through the mazelike arrangement of the centers and tables.

Under this loft is an area large enough for a light table with manipulatives and blocks. The light table can be used in conjunction with the art supplies and some of the sand and water supplies. Colors appear entirely different when placed on the bright light of the table. The loft can be completely open underneath, or partially closed in with plastic walls. The light table can be portable and easily moved to move in the sand, water, or even create another temporary "cozy" area as needed. Temporary curtains can be added to create a puppet stage or lemonade stand. There are so many possibilities!

As in the previous classrooms, I have used a color scheme with neutral, off-white walls and light gray linoleum. The children's artwork is matted with bright construction paper on the walls. The bulletin boards are ever-changing with children's work. There are more areas for the children's work than for the younger ages since more will be done in three-dimensional materials. They also need a space in the block area to display structures for a day or so. Color in furnishings is kept to more neutral colors since the children, their art, and the many toys provide ever-changing colors. Too many different bright colors can be more confusing and add to behavior problems than using basic neutral colors. All the shelves and tables are wood and not added colors. It is very hard to see the true colors of green, orange, and pink when working on a red tabletop. The water and sand tables are clear so the children can see beneath the water as well as in the water. It is much easier to see objects sink or float when looking from the side instead of from the top.

To add another extension to the play in the dramatic, block, and science areas, a talking tube with hollow tubing and funnels could be attached to shelf units or built into some movable table/stations. One could connect the dramatic area to block area, and another could connect the block area to the science area. Perhaps there is a way to attach a talking tube from one loft to another, provided the tube is attached to the ceiling in some way and the lofts are not going to be moved.

Figures A–9 and A–10 show other sample arrangements for a four-year-old classroom.

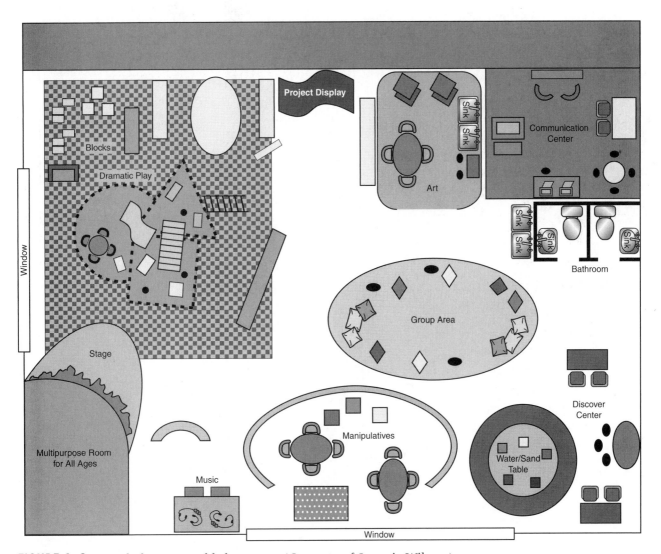

FIGURE A–9 Sample four-year-old classroom. (Courtesy of Jeannie Wilson.)

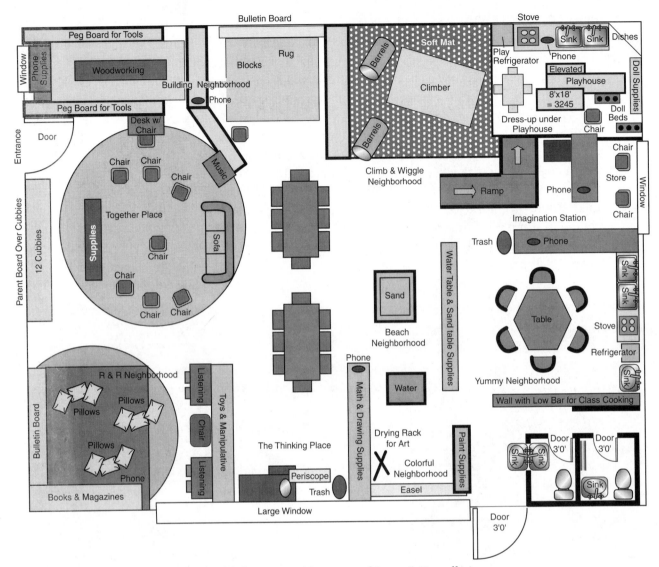

FIGURE A–10 Sample four-year-old classroom. (Courtesy of Irene J. Dowdle.)

Five-Year-Old Classroom

Nancy R. Holland

 With this setting (Figure A–11), I have really thrown away the budget and used imagination and dreams. Once again the walls are an off-white or light gray. The floors are gray linoleum that is easy to care for. Carpets help divide the various activity areas and define space. There is a main entrance, perhaps off of a hallway or maybe from outside. The second doorway leads to the playground area. Another doorway is shown that leads to the bathroom and storage area. Hopefully there will be a special space set aside through this doorway for the teachers. There are eight tall windows spaced around the classroom, letting in lots of natural light. The windows are so the children can observe happenings outside, yet tall enough to spread light throughout the room. There is also a skylight in the center of the room, over the stage (a large group area).

As with the other environments, there is an area of welcome for the children and parents. However, since five-year-olds are a little more independent than younger children, I have put cubbies on each side of the main entrance. As you enter the classroom, you look at the room's center, of which is a large group area that will be referred to as the stage. (This will be explained later.) In front of this area is a cushioned seat with storage underneath. This is a central space between the two sets of cubbies, where parent and child can say good-byes and hellos. The cubbies, soft carpets, plants, and a large, cushioned seat create a small alcove that tells the families that they are welcome. The two small tables labeled sign-in are where the adult and child can sign in together. Many five-year-olds are interested in copying their names if they are not already printing.

The five-year-old classroom seemed a good environment to try the perimeter strategy. The activity areas are spaced around the perimeter of the classroom. After entering on the right you come to the art area. The children have become more independent, now using paints, glue, and scissors. Everything is stored on low, open shelves. More shelf space is needed since more complex projects may be created in this area. This is considered a "messy" area, so it is placed near the sink and bathroom and kept on linoleum. There is an easel as well as a table and space for supplies and even a drying rack. The sink is child size to promote easier child preparation and cleanup. Five-year-olds are eager to please their teachers, and they follow examples and instructions more readily than younger children. After the teacher demonstrates the proper use and care of equipment, the children will become more independent and responsible for the supplies. Plenty of paper towels and sponges are at the sink to assist in cleaning.

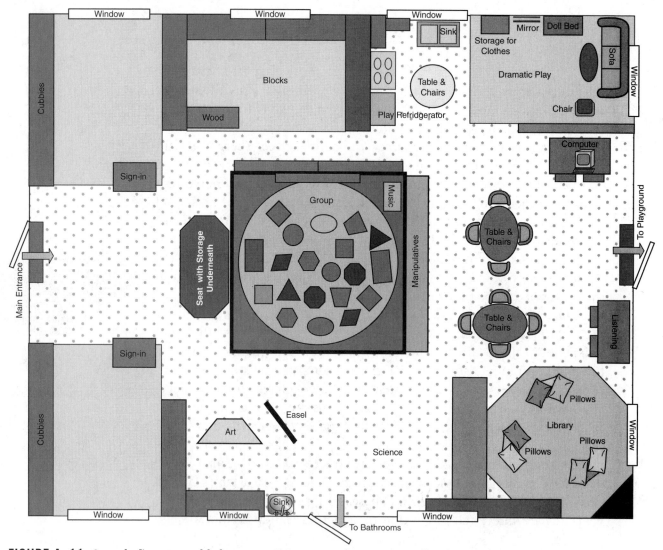

FIGURE A–11 Sample five-year-old classroom. (Courtesy of Nancy R. Holland.)

Next to the art area is the science area. As in previous environments, there are plants and animals to care for. Five-year-olds really enjoy collecting things. They are also at a stage where they form best friends and do things together. Not only is there a double shelf to separate the science and library, there is a small tree house loft that connects the two areas against the wall. The children may climb to the top using a knotted rope that is accessible in the science area. The rope gives children an opportunity to test their muscles and strength, but only if they choose to enter that way. They may choose instead to reach the top by climbing the ladder in the library side. Under the tree house loft, in the science area, is space to rotate sand, water, and light activities. The window gives enough light for experiments and growing plants (or mold projects). There could be a series of different boards (white/wipe-off, cork bulletin, magnetic, felt, and sticky boards) in the loft to record scientific information or write notes. The tree house loft actually appears to be in the trees since a textured trunk and branches extend above the loft. The tree is decorated as needed for each season and may have apples, butterflies, and maybe even a real nest just out of reach. Children could use the binoculars to get a closer look and then have another nest below to examine. The pulley system described in the four-year-old environment could help raise and lower items as needed.

The other entrance to the tree house loft is in the library. The double shelf extends completely under the loft so the two areas are separated. The space under the loft on this side could be used as a puppet stage. The shelves house many books, felt items, and special toys to use to retell the stories, or create your own. This is probably the quietest area in the room, but it is not too quiet since five-year-olds usually prefer the company of one or two other children. There are pillows to cuddle together or stretch out alone. As with all ages, five-year-olds also need a place to be alone. It is not labeled, but the triangle in the corner is the place for one, where a single child can retreat and think about the day or rest. Also in the library is the listening center, which houses books and tapes. This now leads us to one of the larger areas of the room.

Five-year-olds are ready to sort, size, pattern, and create. They work more independently and stay at task longer. Skills are now developing faster, and they are eager to try new things. More manipulative toys are needed than ever before. Four trapezoid tables are used to create two larger tables, or they can be pulled apart to create more seating area. All the manipulatives are in individual, labeled boxes, making it easier to find and replace the toys. There are games, puzzles, counters, small-scale unit and interlocking blocks, and lacing cards. There are boxes with preprinted words and numbers to trace with dry-erase markers, and containers with pencils and paper for writing and drawing. There are boxes with objects to sort, count, categorize and compare. These toys can be used alone or in conjunction with another box of toys. Each box has a photo to help separate and return toys to proper box (another way of sorting).

Close to this area is the computer table. It is backed up to a low divider separating it from the dramatic play area. There are two chairs to encourage working together. (Once I observed a child hand a portable phone from the dramatic play area to a child at the computer. That child obviously had observed someone else talking on the phone and working at the computer, and she was very good at it!)

The dramatic play area is another large area in the classroom. Five-year-olds take a little more time to plan an activity and organize play than younger children. The drawing shows the area as a kitchen and living room with dress-up clothes and a doll bed. The sink is in front of the window, which can be decorated just like at home. Real props are used for play in this area. Part of the floor is covered with a carpet piece, while part is left with the linoleum. A child-size broom and dustpan can be used in the kitchen on the linoleum. The furniture can be moved or turned around to create different scenarios. Small dividers can be added to section it into smaller sections to represent different stores or a café. The sofa and chair can become a waiting room, and the kitchen appliances can be rearranged into a doctor's office. Given the props, the children can set up their own play.

Next to the dramatic play area is the block area. This also is a large area for play. The children have access to a variety of blocks and accessories. Some favorites are the unit blocks, waffle blocks, and large, hollow blocks. Waffle blocks are good for connecting and making enclosures, while unit blocks and hollow blocks can create inclines and ramps. Unit blocks are great for developing math skills. As in the dramatic play area, the older children need more room and a larger amount of time to organize and execute their play with blocks. The woodworking area is included in the block area. It may be used for sawing, hammering, or maybe just as a fix-it shop for broken toys. Five-year-olds like to take things apart and put them back together.

This takes us around the perimeter of the classroom. The center of the room is usually open and easily accessible from all areas of the room. To keep this from being an area where there is running and to create more space, the center of the room is built on a small platform 1 to 2 feet tall. This platform is the area I previously called the stage. The floor is left as linoleum but covered with a circular carpet. On the drawing, you see a line indicating where the floor changes color as a visual warning of the change in height. A small fence may also be used to define the outer edges of the platform. The cushioned seat defines one side of the stage. The manipulative shelves define another side of the stage. On another side the balance beam and other small equipment can sit until needed. On the fourth side facing the bathrooms is a ramp to assist a child that may be in a wheelchair or on crutches.

The drawing shows the stage ready for group time. There are twenty sit-upons on the drawing but I would hope that this could be the classroom where the group size is sixteen with a ratio of 1:8. Perhaps there are extra for the resource teachers and volunteers. Children get their colorful sit-upons out of the cushioned seat/storage area. These sit-upons are made from washable vinyl and are made in the different basic shapes and colors. A portable display unit houses the teacher's books, calendar, and props for the day. When group time is over, the sit-upons are returned to storage and this stage becomes the music/movement area. The portable display can be moved to the edge or even put on the lower floor. Built in storage bins under the stage holds instruments, scarves, letter and number cards, beanbags, and various props for simple games.

Five-year-olds still need a place to hop, jump over low objects, stretch, perform small tricks, practice dance steps, and twirl with a friend. With a few props and the children planning, the stage can become a circus arena or a dance theatre. Leaving the carpet in place will reduce the noise level. The carpet can be removed if the dancing is enhanced by the sound of shoes on linoleum. The balance beam, hula-hoops, and small plastic cones can be put on the stage to create a mini-obstacle course. Five-year-olds are not ready for competition games but do enjoy making up games and creating their own rules.

Another way to use the stage area would be to actually use it as a stage! Invite parents and friends to a special presentation, with the children performing on the stage. The side closest to the main entrance could have a curtain dropped from the ceiling (use the pulleys) to make a backdrop. All the shelves and tables are easily moved, and chairs can be brought in for the adults. There are then three sides where the performance can be viewed. The skylight will give special natural light to the stage during the day, and other lighting can be provided for a night performance.

One other option for the stage is to get a sit-upon or pillow and look up through the skylight at the rain falling softly outside. Put the mountain creek tape on the player and relax! Perhaps it has been a long day. What a way to end it!

Figures A–12 and A–13 show other sample arrangements for a five-year-old classroom.

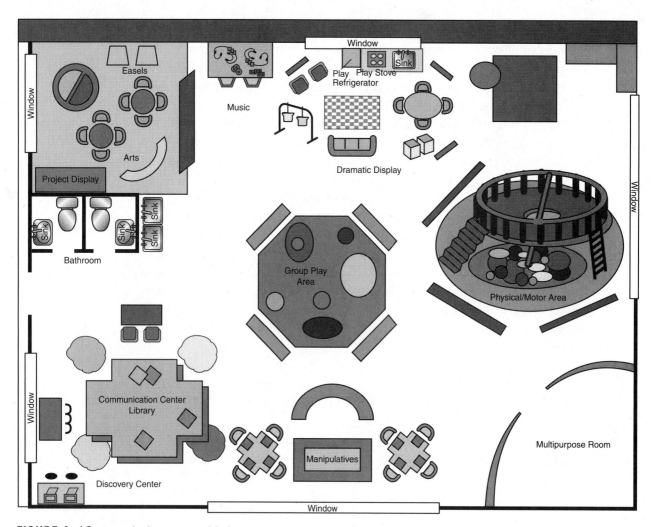

FIGURE A–12 Sample five-year-old classroom. (Courtesy of Jeannie Wilson.)

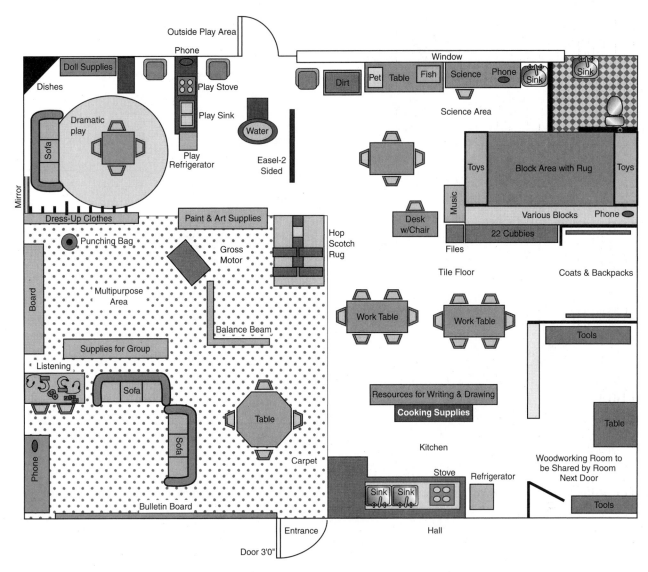

FIGURE A–13 Sample five-year-old classroom. (Courtesy of Irene J. Dowdle.)

Appendix C

National Child Care Organizations

The Administration for Children and Families (ACF)
370 L 'Enfant Promenade SW
Washington, DC 20447
http://www.acf.dhhs.gov

The Child Care Food Program
U.S. Department of Agriculture
Washington, DC 20250
http://www.usda.gov/

The Children's Foundation
725 15th Street NW, Suite 505
Washington, DC 20005-2109
Phone: 202-347-3300
Fax: 202-347-3382
E-mail: info@childrensfoundation.net
http://www.childrensfoundation.net/

Education International (ACEI)
17904 Georgia Avenue, Suite 215
Olney, MD 20832
Phone: 301-570-2111
Toll Free: 1-800-423-3563
Fax: 301-570-2212
E-mail: aceihq@aol.com
http://www.udel.edu/bateman/acei

National Association for Family Day Care
P.O. Box 10373
Des Moines, IA 50306
Toll Free: 1-800-359-3817
E-mail: nafcc@nafcc.org
http://www.nafcc.org

National Association for the Education of Young Children (NAEYC)
1509 16th Street, NW
Washington, DC 20036-1426
http://www.naeyc.org

National Association of Child Care Professionals
P.O. Box 90723
Austin, TX 78709-0723
Phone: 512-301-5557
Toll Free: 1-800-537-1118
Fax: 512-301-5080
E-mail: admin@naccp.org
http://www.naccp.org

National Child Care Association
1016 Rosser Street
Conyers, GA 30012
Toll Free: 1-800-543-7161
http://www.nccanet.org/

National Child Care Information Center

243 Church Street, NW, 2nd Floor
Vienna, VA 22180
Toll Free: 1-800-616-2242
Fax: 1-800-716-2242
TTY: 1-800-516-2242
E-mail: info@nccic.org
http://www.nccic.org

National Head Start Association

1651 Prince Street
Alexandria, VA 22314
Phone: 703-739-0875
Fax: 703-739-0878
http://www.nhsa.org

National Resource Center for Health and Safety in Child Care

UCHSC at Fitzsimons
Campus Mail Stop F541
P.O. Box 6508
Aurora, CO 80045-0508
Toll Free: 1-800-598-KIDS
E-mail: natl.child.res.ctr@uchsc.edu
http://nrc.uchsc.edu

U.S. Department of Health and Human Services

200 Independence Avenue SW
Washington, DC 20201
Phone: 202-619-0257
Toll Free: 1-877-696-6775
E-mail: HHS.Mail@hhs.gov
http://www.hhs.gov

U.S. Small Business Administration

409 3rd Street SW
Washington, DC 20416
Toll Free: 1-800-U-ASK-SBA
http://www.sba.gov

USA National Child Abuse Hotline

For national child abuse information, call the Childhelp USA National Child Abuse Hotline (staffed 24 hours daily with professional crisis counselors): 1-800-4-A-CHILD or 1-800-2-A-CHILD (TDD)

State Contact Information

Alabama

Alabama Department of Human Resources
Childcare Subsidy Program
Family Assistance Division

50 North Ripley Street
Montgomery, AL 36104
Phone: 334-242-1773
Fax: 334-242-0513

Alabama Department of Children's Affairs
Head Start Collaboration Office

RSA Tower, 201 Monroe Street
Montgomery, AL 36130-2755
Phone: 334-223-0502
http://dca.state.al.us/osr/hsco.htm

Department of Human Resources
Office of Child Care Licensing Regulations,
Family Services

50 Ripley Street
Montgomery, AL 36130
Phone: 334-242-1425
Fax: 334-242-0939
http://www.dhr.state.al.us/fsd/licresdv.asp

Childcare Resource Network

P.O. Box 681025
Ft. Payne, AL 35968-1611
Phone: 256-845-8238
Fax: 256-845-6731

Alabama Department of Education

Attn.: State Director, Child Nutrition Programs
Gordon Persons Building
50 North Ripley Street, Room 5301
Montgomery, AL 36130-2101
Phone: 334-242-1988
Fax: 334-242-2475

Alabama Department of Human Resources
Division of Child Support

50 Ripley Street
Montgomery, AL 36130-1801
Phone: 334-242-9300
Fax: 334-242-0606
http://www.dhr.state.al.us/csed/default.asp

U.S. Small Business Administration

801 Tom Martin Drive, Suite 201
Birmingham, AL 35211
Phone: 205-290-7101
Fax: 205-290-7404

———

To report suspected child abuse in Alabama, call any
sheriff's department or any county department of
human resources office.
State Home Page: http://www.state.al.us/
State Child Care Home Page: http://
www.dhr.state.al.us/fad/child_care_sub.asp

Alaska

Alaska Department of Education and Early Development
Division of Early Development

333 West 4th Avenue, Suite 220
Anchorage, AK 99501-2341
Phone: 907-269-4607
Fax: 907-269-4635

Alaska Department of Education and Early Development

Head Start–State Collaboration Office
P.O. Box 112100
Juneau, AK 99811-2100
Phone: 907-465-4861
Fax: 907-465-8638
http://www.eed.state.ak.us/EarlyDev/
headstart.html

Alaska Division of Family and Youth Services

P.O. Box 110630
Juneau, AK 99811-0630
Phone: 907-465-3207
Fax: 907-465-3397 or 907-465-3190
http://www.eed.state.ak.us/EarlyDev/
licensing.html

Child Care Connection

P.O. Box 240008
Anchorage, AK 99524-0008
Phone: 907-563-1966
http://www.eed.state.ak.us/EarlyDev/
ccresource.html

Alaska Department of Education and Early Development

Attn.: State Director, Child Nutrition Programs
801 West 10th Street, Suite 200
Juneau, AK 99801-1894
Phone: 907-465-3316
Fax: 907-463-5279
http://www.eed.state.ak.us/tls/schoolhealth/
nutrition.html

Alaska Child Support Enforcement Division

550 West 7th Avenue, Suite 312
Anchorage, AK 99501-6699
Phone: 907-269-6804
Fax: 907-269-6868
http://www.csed.state.ak.us

U.S. Small Business Administration
Alaska District Office

510 L Street, Suite 310
Anchorage, AK 99501
Phone: 907-271-4022
Fax: 907-271-4545
Toll Free: (outside Anchorage) 1-800-755-7034

———

To report suspected child abuse in Alaska,
call 1-800-478-4444.
State Home Page: http://www.state.ak.us/
State Child Care Home Page: http://
www.eed.state.ak.us/EarlyDev/

American Samoa

American Samoa Department of Human and Social Services
American Samoa

G.P.O. Box 997534
Pago Pago, AS 96799
Phone: 684-633-2696
Fax: 684-633-7449

Arizona

Arizona Department of Economic Security
Child Care Administration

1789 W. Jefferson, 801A
Phoenix, AZ 85007
Phone: 602-542-4248
Fax: 602-542-4197

Arizona Governor's Division for Children
Head Start–State Collaboration Office

1700 West Washington, Suite 101-B
Phoenix, AZ 85007
Phone: 602-542-3483
Fax: 602-542-4644
http://www.governor.state.az.us/children/
e_head.html

Department of Health Services
Office of Child Care Licensure

1647 East Morten, Suite 230
Phoenix, AZ 85020
Phone: 602-674-4220
Fax: 602-861-0674
http://www.hs.state.az.us/als/childcare/index.html

Department of Economic Security

Child Care Administration, Site Code 801A
P.O. Box 6123
1789 W. Jefferson
Phoenix, AZ 85005
Phone: 602-542-4248
Fax: 602-542-4197

Children and Family Services (Southern Arizona)

2800 East Broadway
Tucson, AZ 85716
Phone: 520-881-8940
http://www.arizonachildcare.org

**Association for Supportive Child Care
(Northern and Central Arizona)**

3910 S. Rural Road, Suite O
Tempe, AZ 85282
Phone: 602-736-5935

**Child Care Resource and Referral State Administration
DES/Child Care Administration**

P.O. Box 6123, Site Code 801A
Phoenix, AZ 85005
Phone: 602-542-2575

Arizona State Department of Education

Attn.: State Director, Student Services
1535 West Jefferson Avenue, Bin 7
Phoenix, AZ 85007
Phone: 602-542-8700
Fax: 602-542-3818
http://www.ade.state.az.us/health-safety/
cnp/cacfp/

**Arizona Department of Economic Security
Division of Child Support Enforcement**

P.O. Box 40458, Site Code 021A
Phoenix, AZ 85067
Phone: 602-274-7646
Fax: 602-274-8250
http://www.de.state.az.us/links/dcse/index.html

**U.S. Small Business Administration
Arizona District Office**

2828 North Central Avenue, Suite 800
Phoenix, AZ 85004
Phone: 602-745-7200
Fax: 602-745-7210

To report suspected child abuse in Arizona,
call toll free 1-888-SOS-CHILD (888-767-2445).
State Home Page: http://www.state.az.us/
State Child Care Home Page: http://
www.de.state.az.us/links/chdcare/cca.html

Arkansas

**Arkansas Department of Human Services
Division of Child Care and Early Education**

Donaghey Plaza South MS S140
P.O. Box 1437
Little Rock, AR 72203-1437
Phone: 501-682-4891
Fax: 501-682-4897
http://www.state.ar.us/childcare/

**Arkansas Head Start Association
Head Start–State Collaboration Project**

523 South Louisiana, Suite 301
Little Rock, AR 72201
Phone: 501-371-0740
Fax: 501-370-9109
http://www.arheadstart.org/

**Child Care Licensing Division of Child Care and
Early Childhood Education**

P.O. Box 1437, Slot 720
Little Rock, AR 72203-1437
Phone: 501-682-8590
Fax: 501-682-2317
http://www.state.ar.us/childcare/provinfo.html

**Arkansas Department of Human Services
Division of Child Care and Early Childhood Education**

101 East Capitol, Suite 106
Little Rock, AR 72201
Toll Free: 1-800-445-3316

**Arkansas Department of Human Services
Division of Child Care and Early Childhood Education**

Attn.: State Director, Special Nutrition
Programs
P.O. Box 1437, Slot 705
Little Rock, AR 72203-1437
Phone: 501-682-8869
Fax: 501-682-2234
http://www.state.ar.us/childcare/usda.html

**Arkansas Office of Child Support Enforcement
Department of Finance and Administration
Division of Revenue**

712 West 3rd, P.O. Box 8133
Little Rock, AR 72203
Phone: 501-682-6169
Fax: 501-682-6002
http://www.state.ar.us/dfa/childsupport/
index.html

**U.S. Small Business Administration
Arkansas District Office**

2120 Riverfront Drive, Suite 100

Little Rock, AR 72202
Phone: 501-324-5871
Fax: 501-324-5199

————

To report suspected child abuse in Arkansas, call 1-800-482-5964.
State Home Page: http://www.state.ar.us/
State Child Care Home Page: http://www.state.ar.us/childcare/

California

California State Department of Education
Child Development Division

560 J Street, Suite 220
Sacramento, CA 95814
Phone: 916-322-6233
Fax: 916-323-6853
http://www.cde.ca.gov/cyfsbranch/child_development/

California Department of Education
Child Development Division
Head Start–State Collaboration Office

560 J Street, Suite 220
Sacramento, CA 95814
Phone: 916-323-9727
Fax: 916-323-6853
http://www.cde.ca.gov/cyfsbranch/child_development/CHSSCOview.htm

Department of Social Services
Community Care Licensing Division

744 P Street, Mail Stop 19-50
Sacramento, CA 95814
Phone: 916-324-4031
Fax: 916-323-8352
http://www.ctc.ca.gov/credentialinfo/leaflets/cl797/
cl797.html

California Child Care Resource and
Referral Network

111 New Montgomery Street
San Francisco, CA 94105
Phone: 415-882-0234
Fax: 415-882-6233
http://www.rrnetwork.org/

California Department of Education

Attn.: State Director, Nutrition Services Division
P.O. Box 944272
560 J Street, Room 270
Sacramento, CA 95814
Phone: 916-323-7311
Fax: 916-327-0503
http://www.cde.ca.gov/nsd/ccfp/

California Department of Child Support Services

744 P Street, Mail Stop 17-29
Sacramento, CA 95814
Phone: 916-654-1556
Fax: 916-653-8690
http://www.childsup.cahwnet.gov/Default.htm

U.S. Small Business Administration

455 Market Street, 6th Floor
San Francisco, CA 94105-2420
Phone: 415-744-6820

————

To report suspected child abuse in California, call any state licensing office, any law enforcement office, or any child protective office in any of the county social/health/welfare offices.
State Home Page: http://www.state.ca.us/
State Child Care Home Page:
http://www.cde.ca.gov/cyfsbranch/child_development/
Child Development Division's Care about Quality
Web site: http://www.careaboutquality.org

Colorado

Colorado Department of Human Services
Division of Child Care

1575 Sherman Street
Denver, CO 80203-1714
Phone: 303-866-5958
Fax: 303-866-4453

Colorado Head Start–State Collaboration Project

136 State Capitol Building
Denver, CO 80203
Phone: 303-866-4609
Fax: 303-866-6368

Department of Human Services Division of Child Care

1575 Sherman Street, First Floor
Denver, CO 80203-1714
Phone: 303-866-5958
Fax: 303-866-4453
http://www.cdhs.state.co.us/childcare/home.html

Colorado Office of Resource and Referral Agencies

7853 E. Arapahoe Court, Suite 3300
Englewood, CO 80112-1377
Phone: 303-290-9088
Fax: 303-290-8005
http://www.corra.org

Colorado Department of Public Health and Environment

Attn.: State Director
FCHSD-CAC-A4
4300 Cherry Creek Drive South
Denver, CO 80222-1530
Phone: 303-692-2330
Fax: 303-756-9926
http://www.cdphe.state.co.us/fc/fchom.asp#cacfp

Colorado Department of Human Services Division of Child Support Enforcement

1575 Sherman Street, 2nd Floor
Denver, CO 80203-1714
Phone: 303-839-1203
http://www.childsupport.state.co.us/

U.S. Small Business Administration

721 19th Street, Suite 426
Denver, CO 80202-2517
Phone: 303-844-2607
Fax: 303-844-6468

———

To report suspected child abuse in Colorado, call any county department of social services.
State Home Page: http://www.state.co.us/
State Child Care Home Page: http://www.cdhs.state.co.us/childcare

Connecticut

Connecticut Department of Social Services Family Services/ Child Care Team

25 Sigourney Street, 10th Floor
Hartford, CT 06106-5033
Phone: 860-424-5006
Fax: 860-951-2996

Connecticut Head Start–State Collaboration Office Department of Social Services

25 Sigourney Street
Hartford, CT 06106
Phone: 860-424-5066
Fax: 860-951-2996

Connecticut Department of Public Health Child Day Care Licensing

410 Capitol Avenue
Mail Station 12 DAC
P.O. Box 340308
Hartford, CT 06134-0308
Phone: 860-509-8045
Fax: 860-509-7541
http://www.dph.state.ct.us/BRS/Day_Care/day_care.htm

United Way of Connecticut/ Child Care Infoline

1344 Silas Deane Highway
Rocky Hill, CT 06067
Phone: 860-571-7544
Fax: 860-571-7525
http://www.infoline.org/parents/childcare/default.asp

Connecticut Department of Education

Attn.: State Director, Child Nutrition Programs
25 Industrial Park Road
Middletown, CT 06457-1543
Phone: 860-807-2070
Fax: 860-807-2084

Connecticut Department of Social Services Bureau of Child Support Enforcement

25 Sigourney Street
Hartford, CT 06105-5033
Phone: 860-424-5251
Fax: 860-951-2996
http://www.dss.state.ct.us/csrc/csrc.htm

U.S. Small Business Administration Connecticut District Office

330 Main Street, 2nd Floor
Hartford, CT 06106-1800
Phone: 860-240-4700
Fax: 860-240-4659
TTD: 1-800-877-8845

———

To report suspected child abuse in Connecticut, call 1-800-842-2288 (TDD/hearing impaired: 1-800-624-5518).
State Home Page: http://www.state.ct.us/
State Child Care Home Page: http://www.dss.state.ct.us/ccare/ccare.htm

Washington, DC

District of Columbia Department of Human Services
Office of Early Childhood Development
Commission on Social Service

717 14th Street NW, #730
Washington, DC 20005
Phone: 202-727-1839
Fax: 202-727-8166

District of Columbia
Head Start–State Collaborative Office

717 14th Street NW, Suite 730
Washington, DC 20005
Phone: 202-727-1839
Fax: 202-727-9709

Licensing Regulation Administration
Human Services Facility Division

614 H Street NW, Suite 1003
Washington, DC 20001
Phone: 202-727-7226
Fax: 202-727-7780

Washington Child Development Council

2121 Decatur Place NW
Washington, DC 20008
Phone: 202-387-0002
Fax: 202-332-2834

District of Columbia Public Schools

Attn.: State Director, Division of Logistical
Support, Food Services
3535 V Street NE
Washington, DC 20018-7000
Phone: 202-576-7400
Fax: 202-576-6835

Office of Paternity and Child
Support Enforcement

800 9th Street SW, 2nd Floor
Washington, DC 20024-2480
Phone: 202-645-5330
Fax: 202-645-4123

U.S. Small Business Administration
Washington District Office

1110 Vermont Avenue NW, 9th Floor
Washington, D.C. 20005
(202) 606-4000

To report suspected child abuse in District of
Columbia, call 202-576-6762 (Metropolitan
Police Department). To report suspected neglect,
call 202-727-0995 (Department of Human
Services).
State Home Page: http://www.washingtondc.gov
State Child Care Home Page: http://dhs.dc.gov/
info/earlychildhood.shtm

Delaware

Delaware Department of Health and
Social Services
Lewis Building–Herman Holloway Campus

1901 N. DuPont Highway
P.O. Box 906
New Castle, DE 19720
Phone: 302-577-4880
Fax: 302-577-4405

Delaware Department of Education
CII Branch/ECEC
Head Start–State Collaboration Office

Townsend Building
P.O. Box 1402
Dover, DE 19903-1402
Phone: 302-739-4667
Fax: 302-739-2388

Department of Services for Children,
Youth, and Families
Office of Child Care Licensing

1825 Faulkland Road
Wilmington, DE 19805
Phone: 302-892-5800
Fax: 302-633-5112

The Family and Workplace Connection

3511 Silverside Road, Suite 100
Wilmington, DE 19810
Phone: 302-479-1679
Fax: 302-479-1693
http://www.familyandworkplace.org/

Delaware Department of Public Instruction

Attn.: State Director, School Support Services,
Child Nutrition Programs
Townsend Building
Federal and Lockerman Streets
P.O. Box 1402
Dover, DE 19903-1402
Phone: 302-739-4676
Fax: 302-739-6397

Delaware Department of
Health and Social Services
Division of Child Support Enforcement

1901 N. DuPont Highway, Biggs Building
New Castle, DE 19720
Phone: 302-577-4807
Fax: 302-577-4873
http://www.state.de.us/dhss/dcse/

U.S. Small Business Administration
Delaware District Office

824 N. Market Street
Wilmington, DE 19801-3011
Phone: 302-573-6294
Fax: 302-573-6060

———

To report suspected child abuse in Delaware,
call 1-800-292-9582.
State Home Page: http://www.state.de.us/
State Child Care Home Page: http://
www.state.de.us/dhss/dss/childcare.html

Florida

Florida Partnership for School Readiness

The Holland Building, Room 251
600 S. Calhoun Street
Tallahassee, FL 32399-0001
Phone: 850-488-0337
Fax: 850-922-5188

Florida Partnership for School Readiness
Head Start–State Collaboration Office

The Holland Building, Room 251
600 S. Calhoun Street
Tallahassee, FL 32399
Phone: 850-488-0337
Fax: 850-922-5188

Department of Children and Families
Family Safety and Preservation
Child Care Services

1317 Winewood Boulevard
Building 6, Room 389A
Tallahassee, FL 32399-0700
Phone: 850-488-4900
Fax: 850-488-9584

Florida Children's Forum

2807 Remington Green Circle
Tallahassee, FL 32308
Phone: 850-681-7002
Alt. Phone: 877-FL-CHILD
Fax: 850-681-9816
http://fcforum.org/

Florida Department of Health

Attn.: State Director, Child Food Care Program
2020 Capital Circle SE, Bin A17
Building 5, Room 301
Tallahassee, FL 32399-0700
Phone: 850-488-3875
Fax: 850-414-1622
http://www.doh.state.fl.us/ccfp/

Florida Department of Revenue
Child Support Enforcement Program

P.O. Box 8030
Tallahassee, FL 32314-8030
Phone: 850-488-8733
Fax: 850-488-4401
http://sun6.dms.state.fl.us/dor/childsupport/

U.S. Small Business Administration
South Florida District Office

100 S. Biscayne Boulevard, 7th Floor
Miami, FL 33131
Phone: 305-536-5521
Fax: 305-536-5058

———

To report suspected child abuse in Florida,
call 1-800-96-ABUSE (1-800-962-2873).
State Home Page: http://www.state.fl.us/
State Child Care Home Page:
http://www5.myflorida.com/cf_web/myflorida2/
healthhuman/childcare/
Florida Partnership for School Readiness: http:
//www.myflorida.com/myflorida/government/
governorinitiatives/schoolreadiness/

Georgia

Georgia Department of Human Resources
Child Care and Parent Services Unit
Division of Family and Children Services

Two Peachtree Street NW, Suite 21-293
Atlanta, GA 30303
Phone: 404-657-3438
Fax: 404-657-3489

Georgia Head Start–State Collaboration Office
Georgia Office of School Readiness

10 Park Place South, Suite 200
Atlanta, GA 30303
Phone: 404-656-5957
Fax: 404-651-7184
http://www.osr.state.ga.us/headstart1.html

Department of Human Resources
Office of Regulatory Services,
Child Care Licensing Section

2 Peachtree Street NW
32nd Floor, Room #458
Atlanta, GA 30303-3142
Phone: 404-657-5562
Fax: 404-657-8936
http://www2.state.ga.us/Departments/
DHR/ORS/orsccl.htm

Georgia Association of Child Care
Resource and Referral Agencies

P.O. Box 243
Tifton, GA 31793
Phone: 912-382-9919
Fax: 912-382-3749

Georgia Office of School Readiness

Attn.: State Director
10 Park Place South, Suite 200
Atlanta, GA 30303-2927
Phone: 404-651-7431
Fax: 404-651-7429
http://www.osr.state.ga.us/osrhome.html

Georgia Department of Human Resources
Child Support Enforcement

P.O. Box 38450
Atlanta, GA 30334-0450
Phone: 404-657-3851
Fax: 404-657-3326
http://www.cse.dhr.state.ga.us/

U.S. Small Business Administration
Georgia District Office

233 Peachtree Street NE, Suite 1900
Atlanta, GA 30303
Phone: 404-331-0100

———

To report suspected child abuse in Georgia,
call the Division of Family and Children's Services
at 404-657-7660.
State Home Page: http://www.state.ga.us/
State Child Care Home Page: http://
www2.state.ga.us/Departments/DHR/ORS/
orsccl.htm

Guam

Guam Department of Public Health and Social Services
Government of Guam

P.O. Box 2816
Agana, GU 96910
Phone: 671-735-7102
Fax: 671-734-5910

U.S. Small Business Administration
Guam Branch Office

400 Route 8, Suite 302
First Hawaiian Bank Building
Mongmong, GU 96927
Phone: 671-472-7419
Fax: 671-472-7365

Hawaii

Hawaii Department of Human Services
Benefit, Employment, and Support
Services Division

820 Mililani Street, Suite 606
Honolulu, HI 96813
Phone: 808-586-7050
Fax: 808-586-5229

Hawaii Department of Education
Community Education Center
Hawaii Head Start–State Collaboration Office

634 Pensacola, Room 99-A
Honolulu, HI 96819
Phone: 808-594-0182
Fax: 808-594-0181

Department of Human Services
Benefit, Employment, and Support
Services Division

820 Mililani Street, Suite 606, Haseko Center
Honolulu, HI 96813
Phone: 808-586-7050
Fax: 808-586-5229

PATCH (People Attentive to Children)

2828 Pa'a Street, Suite 3160
Honolulu, HI 96819
Phone: 808-839-1789
Fax: 808-839-1799
http://www.patch-hi.org/

Hawaii State Department of Education

Attn.: State Director, School Food Services Division
1106 Koko Head Avenue
Honolulu, HI 96816
Phone: 808-733-8400
Fax: 808-732-4293

Hawaii Department of Attorney General
Child Support Enforcement Agency

P.O. Box 1860
Honolulu, HI 96805-1860
Phone: 808-587-3695
Fax: 808-587-3716
http://kumu.icsd.hawaii.gov/csea/csea.htm

U.S. Small Business Administration
Hawaii District Office

300 Ala Moana Boulevard
Room 2-235
Box 50207
Honolulu, HI 96850
Phone: 808-541-2990
Fax: 808-541-2976

―――――――

To report suspected child abuse in Hawaii,
call the appropriate Department of
Human Services office:
Oahu: 808-587-5266
Honolulu: 808-622-7111
Wahiawa: 808-959-0669
Maui: 808-242-8418
Kauai: 808-245-3461
State Home Page: http://www.state.hi.us/
State Child Care Home Page:
http://www.state.hi.us/dhs

Idaho

Idaho Department of Health and Welfare
Division of Welfare

450 West State Street, 6th Floor
P.O. Box 83720
Boise, ID 83720-0036
Phone: 208-334-5815
Fax: 208-334-5817

Idaho Head Start Association, Inc.
Head Start–State Collaboration Office

200 North 4th Street, Suite 20
Boise, ID 83702
Phone: 208-345-1182
Fax: 208-345-1163
http://www.idahoheadstartassoc.net/

Department of Health and Welfare
Bureau of Family and Children's Services

450 W. State Street
P.O. Box 83720
Boise, ID 83720-0036
Phone: 208-334-5691
Fax: 208-334-6664
http://www2.state.id.us/dhw/hwgd_www/
contentlist.html

Idaho CareLine Department of Health and Welfare

450 W. State Street, 3rd Floor
P.O. Box 83720
Boise, ID 83720-0036
Toll Free: 1-800-926-2588
TDD: 208-332-7205
http://www2.state.id.us/dhw/hwgd_www/ecic/
CC/Idaho_C8.htm

Idaho Department of Education

Attn.: State Director, Child Nutrition Programs
Len B. Jordan Office Building
650 West State Street
P.O. Box 83720
Boise, ID 83720-0027
Phone: 208-332-6820
Fax: 208-332-6833
http://www.sde.state.id.us/child/

Idaho Department of Health and Welfare
Bureau of Child Support Services

P.O. Box 83720
Boise, ID 83720-0036
Phone: 208-334-5711
Fax: 208-334-0666
http://www2.state.id.us/dhw/childsupport/
index.htm

U.S. Small Business Administration
Boise Idaho District Office

1020 Main Street
Boise, ID 83702
Phone: 208-334-1696
Fax: 208-334-9353

————

To report suspected child abuse in Idaho, call any local Department of Health and Welfare office.
State Home Page: http://www.state.id.us/
State Child Care Home Page: http://www2.state.id.us/dhw/ecic/home.htm

Illinois

Illinois Department of Human Services
Office of Child Care and Family Services

330 Iles Park Place, Suite 270
Springfield, IL 62718
Phone: 217-785-2559
Fax: 217-524-6029

Illinois Department of Human Services
Head Start–State Collaboration Office

10 Collinsville Avenue, Room 203
East St. Louis, IL 62201
Phone: 618-583-2083
Fax: 618-583-2091

Department of Children and Family Services
Bureau of Licensure and Certification

406 East Monroe Street
Station 60
Springfield, IL 62701-1498
Phone: 217-785-2688
Fax: 217-524-3347
http://www.state.il.us/agency/dhs/childcnp.html

Illinois Network of Child Care Resource and Referral Agencies

207 W. Jefferson Street, Suite 503
Bloomington, IL 61701
Phone: 309-829-5327
Fax: 309-828-1808
http://www.ilchildcare.org

Illinois State Board of Education

Attn.: State Director, Nutrition Programs
and Education Services
100 North First Street
Springfield, IL 62777-0001
Phone: 217-782-2491
Fax: 217-524-6124

Illinois Department of Public Aid
Division of Child Support Enforcement

32 W. Randolph Street, Room 923
Chicago, IL 60601
Phone: 217-524-4602
Fax: 217-524-4608
http://www.state.il.us/dpa/html/cs_child_support_news.htm

U.S. Small Business Administration
Illinois District Office

500 W. Madison Street, Suite 1250
Chicago, IL 60661-2511
Phone: 312-353-4528
Fax: 312-886-5688

————

To report suspected child abuse in Illinois, call 1-800-252-2873.
State Home Page: http://www.state.il.us/
State Child Care Home Page: http://www.state.il.us/agency/dhs/childcnp.html

Indiana

Indiana Family and Social Services Administration
Bureau of Child Development

402 W. Washington Street, W392
Indianapolis, IN 46204
Phone: 317-232-1144
Fax: 317-232-7948

Head Start–State Collaboration Office

402 W. Washington Street, Room W461
Indianapolis, IN 46204
Phone: 317-233-6837
Fax: 317-233-4693

Indiana Family and Social Services Administration
Division of Family and Children
Bureau of Child Development–Licensing Unit

P.O Box 7083
Indianapolis, IN 46207
Phone: 317-232-4468 or 317-232-4469
Fax: 317-232-4436
http://www.carefinderindiana.org/

Indiana Family and Social Services Administration
Division of Family and Children
Bureau of Child Development–Licensing Unit

402 W. Washington Street, Room 386
Indianapolis, IN 46204
Phone: 317-232-4521 or 317-232-1660
Fax: 317-232-4436
http://www.carefinderindiana.org/

**Indiana Association for Child Care
Resource and Referral**

3901 N. Meridian, Suite 350
Indianapolis, IN 46208
Phone: 317-924-5202
Fax: 317-924-5102

Indiana Department of Education

Attn.: State Director, Division of School and
Community Nutrition Programs
State House, Room 229
Indianapolis, IN 46204-2798
Phone: 317-232-0850
Fax: 317-232-0855

Indiana Child Support Bureau

402 W. Washington Street, Room W360
Indianapolis, IN 46204
Phone: 317-232-4877
Fax: 317-233-4925
http://www.in.gov/fssa/children/support/
index.html

**U.S. Small Business Administration
Indiana District Office**

429 N. Pennsylvania Street, Suite 100
Indianapolis, IN 46204-1873
Phone: 317-226-7272
TTD: 317-226-5338
FAX: 317-226-7264

———

To report suspected child abuse in Indiana,
call 1-800-562-2407.
State Home Page: http://www.state.in.us/
State Child Care Home Page: http://
www.state.in.us/fssa/children/bcd/

Iowa

Iowa Department of Human Services Division of ACFS

Hoover State Office Building, 5th Floor
Des Moines, IA 50319-0114
Phone: 515-242-5994
Fax: 515-281-4597

**Iowa Department of Education
Bureau of Children, Families, and Community Services
Head Start–State Collaboration Office**

Grimes State Office Building
Des Moines, IA 50319-0146
Phone: 515-242-6024
Fax: 515-242-6019

**Department of Human Services
Adult, Children, and Family Services
Child Day Care Unit**

Hoover State Office Building, 5th Floor
Des Moines, IA 50319-0114
Phone: 515-281-4357; 515-281-5994
Fax: 515-281-4597

Iowa Child Care and Early Education Network

1021 Fleming Building
218 Sixth Avenue
Des Moines, IA 50309
Phone: 515-883-1206
Fax: 515-244-8997
http://users.dwx.com/icceen/

Iowa Department of Education

Attn.: State Director, Food and Nutrition Bureau
Grimes State Office Building
Des Moines, IA 50319-0146
Phone: 515-281-4757
Fax: 515-281-6548

**Iowa Department of Human Services
Economic Assistance, Child Support Recovery Unit**

Hoover State Office Building, 5th Floor
Des Moines, IA 50319-0114
Phone: 515-281-5580
Fax: 515-281-8854
http://www.dhs.state.ia.us/boc/boc.asp

**U.S. Small Business Administration
Des Moines District**

210 Walnut Street, Room 749
Des Moines IA 50309-2186
Phone: 515-284-4422

———

To report suspected child abuse in Iowa,
call 1-800-362-2178.
State Home Page: http://www.state.ia.us/
State Child Care Home Page: http://
www.dhs.state.ia.us/ACFS/ACFS.asp

Kansas

**Kansas Department of Social and
Rehabilitation Services**

Docking State Office Building, Room 681W
915 SW Harrison
Topeka, KS 66612
Phone: 785-296-3349
Fax: 785-296-0146
http://www.srkansas.org/

Kansas Department of Social and Rehabilitation Services
Head Start–State Collaboration Office

Docking State Office Building
915 SW Harrison, Room 651 South
Topeka, KS 66612
Phone: 785-368-6354
Fax: 785-296-0146

Department of Health and Environment
Child Care Licensing and Registration

1000 SW Jackson
Signature State Office Building, Suite 200
Topeka, KS 66612-1274
Phone: 785-296-1270
Fax: 785-296-0803

Kansas Association of Child Care
Resource and Referral Agencies

112 W. Iron
Salina, KS 67401
Phone: 785-823-3343
Fax: 785-823-3385
http://www.kaccrra.org/index.html

Kansas State Board of Education

Attn.: State Director, Nutrition Services
120 East 10th Street
Topeka, KS 66612-1182
Phone: 785-296-2276
Fax: 785-296-1413
http://www.ksbe.state.ks.us/fsims/fsims.html

Kansas Department of Social and Rehabilitation Services
Child Support Enforcement Program

P.O. Box 497
Topeka, KS 66601
Phone: 913-296-3237
Fax: 913-296-5206
http://www.srkansas.org/services/cse.htm

U.S. Small Business Administration
Kansas District Office

271 W. Third Street North, Suite 2500
Wichita, Kansas 67202-1212
Phone: 316-269-6616
Fax: 316-269-6499

———

To report suspected child abuse in Kansas, call 1-800-922-5330.
State Home Page: http://www.accesskansas.org
State Child Care Home Page: http://www.srskansas.org/ees/child_care.htm

Kentucky

Kentucky Cabinet for Families and Children
Department for Community-Based Services
Division of Child Care

275 East Main Street, 3E-B6
Frankfort, KY 40621
Phone: 502-564-2524
Fax: 502-564-2467

Kentucky Head Start–State Collaboration Office

275 East Main Street, 2W-E
Frankfort, KY 40621
Phone: 502-564-8099
Fax: 502-564-9183
http://www.kih.net/kycollaboration

Cabinet for Health Services
Division of Licensing and Regulation

C.H.R. Building
275 East Main Street, 5E-A
Frankfort, KY 40621
Phone: 502-564-2800
Fax: 502-564-6546

Community Coordinated Child Care (4-C)

1215 South Third Street
Louisville, KY 40203
Phone: 502-636-1358
Fax: 502-636-1488
http://www.4cforkids.org/

Kentucky Cabinet for Human Resources
Division of Child Support Enforcement

275 East Main Street
Frankfort, KY 40621
Phone: 502-564-2285
Fax: 502-564-5988

Kentucky Department of Education

Attn.: State Director, Division of School
and Community Nutrition
500 Mero Street
Frankfort, KY 40601
Phone: 502-573-4390
Fax: 502-573-6775
http://www.kde.state.ky.us/odss/nutrition/default.asp

U.S. Small Business Administration

Romano Mazzoli Federal Building
Kentucky District Office
600 Dr. MLK Jr. Place
Louisville, KY 40202
Phone: 502-582-5761

To report suspected child abuse in Kentucky, call 1-800-752-6200.
State Home Page: http://www.state.ky.us/
State Child Care Home Page: http://cfc.state.ky.us/help/child_care.asp

Louisiana

Louisiana Department of Social Services
Child Care Assistance Program
Office of Family Support, FIND Work/
Child Care Division

P.O. Box 91193
Baton Rouge, LA 70821-9193
Phone: 225-342-9106
Fax: 225-342-9111
http://www.dss.state/la.us/offofs/html/child_care_assistance.html

Louisiana Head Start–State Collaboration Office

412 Fourth Street, Suite 101
Baton Rouge, LA 70802-5212
Phone: 225-219-4245
Fax: 225-219-4248
http://www.dss.state.la.us/offofs/html/head_start_collaboration_proje.html

Department of Social Services Bureau of Licensing

P.O. Box 3078
Baton Rouge, LA 70821
Phone: 504-922-0015
Fax: 504-922-0014
http://www.dss.state.la.us/offofs/html/child_care_assistance.html

Agenda for Children

1326 Josephine Street
P.O. Box 51837
New Orleans, LA 70151
Phone: 504-586-8509
Fax: 504-586-8522
http://www.agendaforchildren.org/

Louisiana Department of Education

Attn.: State Director, Food and Nutrition Services
655 North Fifth Street
P.O. Box 94064
Baton Rouge, LA 70804-9064
Phone: 504-342-3720
Fax: 504-342-3305

Louisiana Office of Family Support
Support Enforcement Services

P.O. Box 94065
Baton Rouge, LA 70804-4065
Phone: 504-342-4780
Fax: 504-342-7397

U.S. Small Business Administration
Louisiana District Office

365 Canal Street, Suite 2820
New Orleans, LA 70130
Phone: 504-589-6685

To report suspected child abuse in Louisiana, call any local child protective agency.
State Home Page: http://www.state.la.us/
State Child Care Home Page: http://www.dss.state.la.us/offofs/html/child_care assistance.html

Maine

Maine Department of Human Services
Office of Child Care and Head Start

11 State House Station
Augusta, ME 04333-0011
Phone: 207-287-5060
Fax: 207-287-5031

Department of Human Services
Office of Child Care and Head Start
Head Start–State Collaboration Office

11 State House Station
Augusta, ME 04333-0011
Phone: 207-287-5060
Fax: 207-287-5031

Bureau of Child and Family Services

221 State Street
Augusta, ME 04333
Phone: 207-287-5060
Fax: 207-287-5031

Child Care Connections

307 Cumberland Avenue
Portland, ME 04104
Phone: 207-775-6503
Fax: 207-775-7327

Maine Department of Human Services

Attn.: State Director, Child and Adult Food Care Program, Division of Purchased and Support Services
221 State House Station
Augusta, ME 04333
Phone: 207-287-5060
Fax: 207-287-5282

Maine Department of Human Services
Bureau of Income Maintenance
Division of Support Enforcement and Recovery

11 State House Station
Augusta, ME 04333
Phone: 207-287-2866
Fax: 207-287-5096

U.S. Small Business Administration
Maine District Office

40 Western Avenue
Augusta, ME 04330
Phone: 207-622-8274
Fax: 207-622-8277

———

To report suspected child abuse in Maine,
call 1-800-452-1999.
State Home Page: http://www.state.me.us/
State Child Care Home Page: http://
www.state.me.us/dhs/

Maryland

Maryland Department of Human Resources
Child Care Administration

311 W. Saratoga Street, 1st Floor
Baltimore, MD 21201
Phone: 410-767-7128
Fax: 410-333-8699
http://www.dhr.state.md.us/cca-home.htm

Department of Human Resources
Office of Licensing
Child Care Administration

311 W. Saratoga Street, 1st Floor
Baltimore, MD 21201
Phone: 410-767-7805
Fax: 410-333-8699

Maryland Head Start–State Collaboration Office
Governor's Office for Children,
Youth and Families

301 West Preston Street, 15th Floor
Baltimore, MD 21201
Phone: 410-767-4196
Fax: 410-333-5248
http://www.ocyf.state.md.us/2g.htm

Maryland Committee for Children, Inc.

608 Water Street
Baltimore, MD 21202
Phone: 410-752-7588
Fax: 410-752-6286
http://mdchildcare.org/mdcfc/mcc.html

Maryland State Department of Education

Attn.: State Director, Nutrition and
Transportation Services
200 West Baltimore Street, 3rd Floor
Baltimore, MD 21201-2595
Phone: 410-767-0199
Fax: 410-333-2635
http://www.msde.state.md.us/programs/
foodandnutrition/childfood.html

Maryland Child Support Enforcement Program

311 West Saratoga Street
Baltimore, MD 21201
Phone: 800-332-6347
Fax: 410-333-8992
http://www.dhr.state.md.us/csea/index.htm

U.S. Small Business Administration
Baltimore District Office

City Crescent Building, 6th Floor
10 South Howard Street
Baltimore, MD 21201
Phone: 410-962-4392
Fax: 410-962-1805

———

To report suspected child abuse in Maryland,
call 1-800-332-6347.
State Home Page: http://www.mec.state.md.us/
State Child Care Home Page: http://
www.dhr.state.md.us/cca-home.htm

Massachusetts

Massachusetts Office of Child Care Services

One Ashburton Place, Room 1105
Boston, MA 02108
Phone: 617-626-2000
Fax: 617-626-2028
http://www.qualitychildcare.org/

Executive Office of Health and Human Services
Head Start–State Collaboration Office

One Ashburton Place, Room 1109
Boston, MA 02108
Phone: 617-727-7600
Fax: 617-727-1396

Office of Child Care Services Licensing

One Ashburton Place, Room 1105
Boston, MA 02108
Phone: 617-727-8900
Fax: 617-626-2028
http://www.qualitychildcare.org/licensing.shtml

Child Care Resource Center

130 Bishop Allen Drive
Cambridge, MA 02139
Phone: 617-547-1063

Massachusetts Department of Education

Attn.: State Director, Nutrition Programs and
Services
350 Main Street
Malden, MA 02351
Phone: 781-388-6479
Fax: 781-388-3399
http://www.doe.mass.edu/cnp/

**Massachusetts Department of Revenue
Child Support Enforcement Division**

141 Portland Street
Cambridge, MA 02139-1937
Phone: 617-577-7200
Fax: 617-621-4991

**U.S. Small Business Administration
Massachusetts District Office**

10 Causeway Street, Room 265
Boston, MA 02222-1093
Phone: 617-565-5590
Fax: 617-565-5598

To report suspected child abuse in Massachusetts,
call 1-800-792-5200.
State Home Page: http://www.state.ma.us/
State Child Care Home Page: http://www.qualitych
ildcare.org/

Michigan

**Michigan Family Independence Agency
Child Development and Care Division**

235 South Grand Avenue, Suite 1302
P.O. Box 30037
Lansing, MI 48909-7537
Phone: 517-373-0356
Fax: 517-241-7843

**Michigan Family Independence Agency
Head Start–State Collaboration Project**

235 South Grand Avenue, Suite 1302
P.O. Box 30037
Lansing, MI 48909
Phone: 517-335-3610
Fax: 517-241-9033

**Department of Consumer and Industry Services
Division of Child Day Care Licensing**

7109 W. Saginaw, 2nd Floor
P.O. Box 30650
Lansing, MI 48909-8150
Phone: 517-373-8300
Fax: 517-335-6121
http://www.cis.state.mi.us/brs/cdc/home.htm

**Michigan 4C Association
(Child Care Food Program Agency)**

2875 Northwind Drive, #200
East Lansing, MI 48823
Phone: 517-351-4171

Michigan Department of Education

Attn.: State Director, School Management Services
P.O. Box 30008
Lansing, MI 48909
Phone: 517-373-8642
Fax: 517-373-4022
http://www.state.mi.us/mde/off/oss/index.
htm#FoodNutrition

**Michigan Department of Social Services
Office of Child Support**

P.O. Box 30478
Lansing, MI 48909-7978
Phone: 517-373-7570
Fax: 517-373-4980

**U.S. Small Business Administration
Michigan District Office**

477 Michigan Avenue, Suite 515,
McNamara Building
Detroit, MI 48226
Phone: 313-226-6075
Fax: 313-226-4769
E-mail: michigan@sba.gov

To report suspected child abuse in Michigan,
call 1-800-942-4357
State Home Page: http://www.state.mi.us/
State Child Care Home Page: http://
www.mfia.state.mi.us/chldDevCare/cdc1.htm

Minnesota

Minnesota Department of Children, Families, and Learning

1500 Highway 36 West
Roseville, MN 55113-4266
Phone: 651-582-8562
Fax: 651-582-8496
http://www.educ.state.mn.us/

Minnesota Department of Children, Families, and Learning Head Start–State Collaboration Office

1500 Highway 36 West
Roseville, MN 55113
Phone: 651-582-8405
Fax: 651-582-8491
http://cfl.state.mn.us/OEO/head_start.htm

Department of Human Services Division of Licensing

444 Lafayette Road
St. Paul, MN 55155-3842
Phone: 561-296-3971
Fax: 561-297-1490
http://www.dhs.state.mn.us/Licensing/ChildCare/default.htm

Minnesota CCR&R Network

380 E. Lafayette Road, Suite 103
St. Paul, MN 55107
Phone: 651-290-9704
Fax: 651-290-9785
http://www.mnchildcare.org/

Minnesota Department of Children, Families, and Learning

Attn.: State Director, Food and Nutrition Services
1500 Highway 36 West
Roseville, MN 55113-4266
Phone: 651-582-8526
Fax: 651-582-8500
http://fns.state.mn.us/

Minnesota Department of Human Services Office of Child Support Enforcement

444 Lafayette Road, 4th Floor
St. Paul, MN 55155-3846
Phone: 612-297-8232
Fax: 612-297-4450

U.S. Small Business Administration Minnesota District Office

100 N. Sixth Street, Suite 210-C Butler Square
Minneapolis, Minnesota 55403
Phone: 612-370-2324
Fax: 612-370-2303

To report suspected child abuse in Minnesota, call 612-296-3971 or any county child protection director.
State Home Page: http://www.state.mn.us/
State Child Care Home Page: http://cfl.state.mn.us/ecfi/

Mississippi

Mississippi Department of Human Services Office for Children and Youth

750 North State Street
Jackson, MS 39202
Phone: 601-359-4544
Fax: 601-359-4422

Mississippi Department of Human Services Office for Children and Youth Head Start–State Collaboration Office

750 North State Street
Jackson, MS 39202
Phone: 601-359-4553
Fax: 601-359-4422
http://www.mdhs.state.ms.us/ocy_hsco.html

Department of Health Division of Child Care

P.O. Box 1700
Jackson, MS 39215-1700
Phone: 601-576-7613
Fax: 601-576-7813

Mississippi Forum on Children and Families

737 North President Street
Jackson, MS 39202
Phone: 601-355-4911
Fax: 601-355-4813
http://www.mfcf.org/

Mississippi Department of Education

Attn.: State Director, Bureau of Child Nutrition
550 High Street, Suite 1601
P.O. Box 771
Jackson, MS 39205-0771
Phone: 601-354-7015
Fax: 601-354-7595

Mississippi Department of Human Services Division of Child Support Enforcement

P.O. Box 352
Jackson, MS 39205
Phone: 601-359-4863
Fax: 601-359-4415

U.S. Small Business Administration
Mississippi District Office

AmSouth Bank Plaza
210 E. Capitol Street, Suite 900
Jackson, MS 39201
Phone: 601-965-4378
Fax: 601-965-5629 or 601-965-4294

———————

To report suspected child abuse in Mississippi,
call 1-800-222-8000.
State Home Page: http://www.state.ms.us
State Child Care Home Page: http://
www.mdhs.state.ms.us/ocy.html

Missouri

Missouri Department of Social Services
Division of Family Services
Income Maintenance

P.O. Box 88
Jefferson City, MO 65103
Phone: 573-751-3221
Fax: 573-751-0507

Missouri Head Start–State Collaboration Office
University of Missouri

31 Stanley Hall
Columbia, MO 65211-6280
Phone: 573-884-0579
Fax: 573-884-0598
http://www.moheadstart.org/

Department of Health
Bureau of Child Care, Safety, and Licensure

1715 Southridge
Jefferson City, MO 65109
Phone: 573-751-2450
Fax: 573-526-5345
http://www.health.state.mo.us/LicensingAnd
Certification/welcome.html

Child Day Care Association

4236 Lindell Boulevard, Suite 300
St. Louis, MO 63108
Phone: 314-351-1412
Alt. Phone: 800-467-CDCA
Fax: 314-531-4184

Missouri Department of Health

Attn.: State Director, Bureau of Food Programs and
Nutrition Education
P.O. Box 570, 930 Wildwood
Jefferson City, MO 65102-0570
Phone: 573-751-6269
Fax: 573-526-3679
http://www.health.state.mo.us/NutritionServices/
EatForHealth.html

Missouri Department of Social Services
Division of Child Support Enforcement

P.O. Box 1527
Jefferson City, MO 65102-1527
Phone: 573-751-1374
Fax: 573-751-8450
http://www.dss.state.mo.us/cse/index.htm

U.S. Small Business Administration
St. Louis District Office

815 Olive Street, Room 242
St. Louis, MO 63101
Phone: 314-539-6600
Fax: 314-539-3785

———————

To report suspected child abuse in Missouri,
call 1-800-392-3738.
State Home Page: http://www.state.mo.us
State Child Care Home Page: http://
www.dss.state.mo.us/dfs/early/index.htm

Montana

Montana Department of Public Health
and Human Services
Human and Community Services Division
Early Childhood Services Bureau

P.O. Box 202952
Helena, MT 59620-2952
Phone: 406-444-1828
Fax: 406-444-2547

Head Start–State Collaboration Office

P.O. Box 202952
Helena, MT 59620-2952
Phone: 406-444-0589
Fax: 406-444-2547

Department of Public Health and
Human Services (DPHHS)
Quality Assurance Division (QAD) Licensing Bureau
Child Care Licensing Program

P.O. Box 202953
Helena, MT 59620-2953
http://www.dphhs.state.mt.us/divisions/qad/
qad.htm

Montana Child Care Resource and Referral Network

c/o Child Care Resources
127 East Main, Suite 314
Missoula, MT 59801
Phone: 406-728-6446
Alt. Phone: 800-728-6446
http://www.childcareresources.org/

Montana Department of Public Health and Human Services

Attn.: State Director, Children's Services
Cogswell Building, 1400 Broadway
P.O. Box 8005
Helena, MT 59604
Phone: 406-444-1828
Fax: 406-444-5956

Department of Social and Rehabilitation Services Child Support Enforcement Division

P.O. Box 202943
Helena, MT 59620
Phone: 406-442-7278
Fax: 406-442-1370

U.S. Small Business Administration Montana District Office

Federal Building
10 West 15th Street, Suite 1100
Helena, MT 59626

To report suspected child abuse in Montana, call 1-800-332-6100.
State Home Page: http://www.state.mt.us/
State Child Care Home Page: http://www.dphhs.state.mt.us/divisions/hcs/hcs.htm

Mariana Islands

Northern Mariana Islands State Board of Education

CNMI P.O. Box 1370 CK
Saipan MP 96950
Phone: 670-664-3714
Fax: 670-664-3717

Nebraska

Nebraska Health and Human Services System Child Care

P.O. Box 95044
Lincoln, NE 68509-5044
Phone: 402-471-9676
Fax: 402-471-7763

Nebraska Head Start–State Collaboration Office Nebraska Department of Education, Office of Children and Families

301 Centennial Mall South
P.O. Box 94987
Lincoln, NE 68509-4987
Phone: 402-471-3501
Fax: 402-471-0117
http://www.nde.state.ne.us/ECH/HeadStart/HSSCP.html

Nebraska Department of Health and Human Services Child Care

P.O. Box 95044
Lincoln, NE 68509-5044
Phone: 402-471-7763
Fax: 402-471-9455
http://www.hhs.state.ne.us/crl/childcare.htm

Midwest Child Care Association

5015 Dodge Street
Omaha, NE 68132
Phone: 402-558-6794

Nebraska Department of Education

Attn.: State Director, Child Nutrition Programs
301 Centennial Mall South
Lincoln, NE 68509-4987
Phone: 402-471-3566
Fax: 402-471-4407
http://www.nde.state.ne.us/NS/index.htm

Nebraska Department of Health and Human Services Child Support Enforcement Office

P.O. Box 94728
Lincoln, NE 68509-4728
Phone: 402-479-5555
Fax: 402-479-5145
http://www.hhs.state.ne.us/cse/cseindex.htm

U.S. Small Business Administration

11145 Mill Valley Road
Omaha, NE 68154
Phone: 402-221-4691
Fax: 402-221-3680

To report suspected child abuse in Nebraska, call 1-800-652-1999.
State Home Page: http://www.state.ne.us/
State Child Care Home Page: http://www.hhs.state.ne.us/chc/chcindex.htm

Nevada

Nevada Department of Human Resources Welfare Division

1470 E. College Parkway
Carson City, NV 89706
Phone: 775-684-0500
Fax: 775-684-0617
http://www.welfare.state.nv.us/welfare.htm

Nevada Head Start–State Collaboration Office
Nevada Department of Human Resources,
Community Connections

3987 South McCarran Boulevard
Reno, NV 89502
Phone: 702-688-2284 x227
Fax: 702-688-2558
http://www.nvcommunityconnections.com/
programs/
programs.php?programid=1

Department of Human Resources
Division of Child and Family Services
Bureau of Child Care Licensing

3920 E. Idaho Street
Elko, NV 89801
Phone: 775-753-1237
Fax: 775-753-2111

Nevada Department of Education

Attn.: State Director, Health and Safety Programs
700 East Fifth Street
Carson City, NV 89701-5096
Phone: 702-687-9154
Fax: 702-687-9199

Nevada State Welfare Division
Child Support Enforcement Program

2527 N. Carson Street, Capitol Complex
Carson City, NV 89710
Phone: 702-687-4744
Fax: 702-684-8026

U.S. Small Business Administration
Nevada District Office

300 Las Vegas Boulevard South, Suite 1100
Las Vegas, NV 89101
Phone: 702-388-6611
Fax: 702-388-6469

To report suspected child abuse in Nevada,
call 1-800-992-5757.
State Home Page: http://www.state.nv.us/
State Child Care Home Page: http://
www.welfare.state.nv.us

New Hampshire

New Hampshire Department of
Health and Human Services
Division for Children, Youth and Families
Bureau of Child Development

129 Pleasant Street
Concord, NH 03301-3857
Phone: 603-271-8153
Fax: 603-271-7982

New Hampshire Head Start–State
Collaboration Office
New Hampshire Department of
Health and Human Services
Child Development Bureau

129 Pleasant Street
Concord, NH 03301-6505
Phone: 603-271-4454
Fax: 603-271-7982

New Hampshire Department of
Health and Human Services
Office of Program Support
Bureau of Child Care Licensing

129 Pleasant Street
Concord, NH 03301
Phone: 603-271-4624
Fax: 603-271-4782

FamilyWorks/Child and Family Services

500 Amherst Street
Nashua, NH 03063
Phone: 603-889-7189
Fax: 603-889-7104

New Hampshire Department of Education

Attn.: State Director, Nutrition Programs and
Services Bureau
101 Pleasant Street
Concord, NH 03301
Phone: 603-271-3860
Fax: 603-271-1953

Health and Human Services Building
Office of Program Support, Office of Child Support

6 Hazen Drive
Concord, NH 03301
Phone: 603-271-4287
Fax: 603-271-4787

U.S. Small Business Administration

143 N. Main Street
Concord, NH 03301
Phone: 603-225-1400
Fax: 603-225-1409

To report suspected child abuse in New Hampshire,
call 1-800-894-5533.
State Home Page: http://www.state.nh.us/
State Child Care Home Page: http://
www.dhhs.state.nh.us/
New Hampshire Child Care Association: http:
//www.nhcca.com

New Jersey

New Jersey Department of Human Services
Division of Family Development

P.O. Box 716
Trenton, NJ 08625
Phone: 609-588-2163
Fax: 609-588-3051

New Jersey Department of Human Services

P.O. Box 700
Trenton, NJ 08625-0700
Phone: 609-984-5321
Fax: 609-292-1903
http://www.state.nj.us/humanservices

Division of Youth and Family Services
Bureau of Licensing

P.O. Box 717
Trenton, NJ 08625-0717
Phone: 609-292-1018
Fax: 609-292-6976

MARO, USDA, FNS, SNP

Attn.: Regional Director
Mercer Corporate Park
300 Corporate Boulevard
Robbinsville, NJ 08691-1598
Phone: 609-259-5050
Fax: 609-259-5128

NJACCRRA

c/o Office for Children
21 Main Street, #114
Hackensack, NJ 07601
Phone: 201-646-3694

New Jersey State Department of Agriculture

Attn.: State Director, Bureau of Child Nutrition
Programs
33 West State Street, 4th Floor
P.O. Box 334
Trenton, NJ 08625-0334
Phone: 609-984-0692
Fax: 609-984-0878

New Jersey Department of Human Services
Division of Family Development
Bureau of Child Support and Paternity Programs

CN 716
Trenton, NJ 08625-0716
Phone: 609-588-2402
Fax: 609-588-3369

U.S. Small Business Administration
New Jersey District Office

Two Gateway Center, 15th Floor
Newark, New Jersey 07102
Phone: 973-645-2434

To report suspected child abuse in New Jersey,
call 1-800-792-8610 (TDD/hearing impaired:
1-800-835-5510).
State Home Page: http://www.state.nj.us/
State Child Care Home Page: http://
www.state.nj.us/humanservices/dfd/chldca.html

New Mexico

New Mexico Department of Children,
Youth, and Families
Child Care Services Bureau

P.O. Drawer 5160, PERA Building, Room 111
Santa Fe, NM 87502-5160
Phone: 505-827-9932
Fax: 505-827-7361

New Mexico Department of Children,
Youth, and Families
Head Start–State Collaboration Office

P.O. Drawer 5160, PERA Building, Room 111
Santa Fe, NM 87502-5160
Phone: 505-827-9952
Fax: 505-827-7361

Child Services Unit / Licensing

P.O. Drawer 5160, PERA Building, Room 111
Santa Fe, NM 87502-5160
Phone: 505-827-4185
Fax: 505-827-7361

YWCA/Carino CCR&R

303 San Mateo Blvd., NE #201
Albuquerque, NM 87108
Phone: 505-265-8565
Alt. Phone: 505-265-8500
Fax: 505-265-8501

New Mexico Children, Youth, and
Families Department

Attn.: State Director, Family Nutrition Bureau
1422 Paseo De Peralta, Building 2
P.O. Box 5160
Santa Fe, NM 87502-5160
Phone: 505-827-9961
Fax: 505-827-9957

New Mexico Human Services Department
Child Support Enforcement Bureau

P.O. Box 25109
Santa Fe, NM 73512
Phone: 505-827-7200
Fax: 505-827-7285

U.S. Small Business Administration
Albuquerque, New Mexico District Office

625 Silver SW, Suite 320
Albuquerque, NM 87102
Phone: 505-346-7909
Fax: 505-346-6711

———

To report suspected child abuse in New Mexico, call 1-800-797-3260.
State Home Page: http://www.state.nm.us/
State Child Care Home Page: http://www.newmexicokids.org/

New York

New York State Department of Family Assistance
Office of Children and Family Services
Bureau of Early Childhood Services

40 North Pearl Street, 11B
Albany, NY 12243
Phone: 518-474-9324
Fax: 518-474-9617

New York State Council on Children and Families
Head Start–State Collaboration Office

5 Empire State Plaza, Suite 2810
Albany, NY 12223-1553
Phone: 518-474-6294
Fax: 518-473-2570
http://capital.net/com/council/headstart.html

New York State Department of Family Assistance
Office of Children and Family Services
Bureau of Early Childhood Services

52 Washington Street, 3N
Rensselaer, NY 12144
Phone: 518-474-9454
Fax: 518-474-9617
http://www.ocfs.state.ny.us/main/becs/default.htm

New York State Child Care Coordinating Council
(Child Care Food Program Agency)

130 Ontario Street
Albany, NY 12206
Phone: 518-463-8663

New York State Department of Health

Attn.: Director
DON-CACFP

Riverview Center
150 Broadway, FL6 West
Albany, NY 12204-2719
Phone: 518-402-7400
Fax: 518-402-7252

New York Department of Social Services
Office of Child Support Enforcement

P.O. Box 14
Albany, NY 12260-0014
Phone: 518-474-9081
Fax: 518-486-3127

———

For callers from the five boroughs of New York City: Manhattan, Queens, Brooklyn, Bronx, and Staten Island

New York City Department of Health
Bureau of Day Care

2 Lafayette Street, 22nd Floor
New York, NY 10007
Phone: 212-676-2444 (212-280-9251 for family child care registration only)
Fax: 212-676-2424
http://www.nyc.gov/html/doh/html/dc/dc.html

U.S. Small Business Administration

26 Federal Plaza, Suite 3100
New York, NY 10278
Phone: 212-264-2454
Fax: 212-264-7751

———

To report suspected child abuse in New York, call 1-800-342-3720.
State Home Page: http://www.state.ny.us
State Child Care Home Page: http://www.ocfs.state.ny.us/main/becs/default.htm

North Carolina

North Carolina Department of
Health and Human Services
Division of Child Development

P.O. Box 29553
Raleigh, NC 27626-0553
Phone: 919-662-4543
Fax: 919-662-4568
http://www.dhhs.state.nc.us/dcd/

North Carolina Head Start–State Collaboration Office

2201 Mail Service Center
Raleigh, NC 27626-2201
Phone: 919-662-4543
Fax: 919-662-4568
http://www.dhhs.state.nc.us/dcd/whatwedo.htm#HS

Division of Child Development
Regulatory Services Section

2201 Mail Service Center
Raleigh, NC 27626-2201
Phone: 919-662-4499 or 919-662-4527 or 800-859-0829 (in-state calls only)
Fax: 919-661-4845
http://www.dhhs.state.nc.us/dcd/provider.htm

North Carolina Child Care Resource and
Referral Network

460 Bayberry Drive
Chapel Hill, NC 27514
Phone: 919-933-5090
Fax: 919-933-0450

North Carolina Health and Human Services Section

Attn.: State Director, Nutrition Services Section
1330 St. Mary's Street
P.O. Box 10008
Raleigh, NC 27608
Phone: 919-715-0636
Fax: 919-733-1384

North Carolina Department of Human Resources
Division of Social Services
Child Support Enforcement Section

100 East Six Forks Road
Raleigh, NC 27609-7750
Phone: 919-420-7982
Fax: 919-571-4126

U.S. Small Business Administration
North Carolina District Office

200 N. College Street, Suite A2015
Charlotte, NC 28202
Phone: 704-344-6563
Fax: 704-344-6769

———

To report suspected child abuse in North Carolina, call CARE-LINE: 1-800-662-7030.
State Home Page: http://www.ncgov.com/
State Child Care Home Page: http://www.dhhs.state.nc.us/dcd/index.htm

North Dakota

North Dakota Department of Human Services
Office of Economic Assistance
State Capitol Judicial Wing

600 East Boulevard
Bismarck, ND 58505-0250
Phone: 701-328-4603
Fax: 701-328-2359

North Dakota Department of Human Services
Head Start–State Collaboration Office

600 East Boulevard
Bismarck, ND 58505
Phone: 701-328-1711
Fax: 701-328-3538
http://www.headstartnd.com/

Department of Human Services
Early Childhood Services

600 East Boulevard
State Capitol Building
Bismarck, ND 58505-0250
Phone: 701-328-4809
Fax: 701-328-3538

Lutheran Social Service of North Dakota

615 S. Broadway, Suite L3
Minot, ND 58701-4473
Phone: 701-838-7800
Alt. Phone: 1-800-450-7801
http://www.lssnd.org/program08.html

North Dakota Department of Public Instruction

Attn.: State Director, Child Nutrition and Food Distribution
600 East Boulevard
Bismarck, ND 58505-0440
Phone: 701-328-2294
Fax: 701-328-2461
http://www.dpi.state.nd.us/dpi/child/index.htm

North Dakota Department of Human Services
Child Support Enforcement Agency

P.O. Box 7190
Bismarck, ND 58507-7190
Phone: 701-328-3582
Fax: 701-328-6575

U.S. Small Business Administration
North Dakota District Office

657 Second Avenue North, Room 219
P.O. Box 3086
Fargo, ND 58108
Phone: 701-239-5131
TDD: 701-239-5657
Fax: 701-239-5645
E-mail: north.dakota@sba.gov

———

To report suspected child abuse in North Dakota, call 1-800-245-3736.
State Home Page: http://www.state.nd.us/
State Child Care Home Page: http://lnotes.state.nd.us/dhs/dhsweb.nsf/ServicePages/ChildrenandFamilyServices

Ohio

**Ohio Department of Human Services
Bureau of Child Care Services**

65 E. State Street, 5th Floor
Columbus, OH 43215
Phone: 614-466-1043
Fax: 614-728-6803

**Ohio Head Start–State Collaboration Office
Ohio Family and Children First
Office of the Governor**

17 South High Street, Suite 550
Columbus, OH 43215
Phone: 614-752-4044
Fax: 614-728-9441
http://www.ohiofcf.org/

**Ohio Department of Job and Family Services
Bureau of Child Care and Development**

255 East Main Street, 3rd Floor
Columbus, OH 43215-5222
Phone: 614-466-1043
Fax: 614-728-6803
http://www.state.oh.us/odhs/cdc/index.htm

Ohio Child Care Resource and Referral Association

c/o Action for Children
78 Jefferson Avenue
Columbus, OH 43215
Phone: 614-224-0222
Fax: 614-224-5437
http://www.occrra.org/

Ohio Department of Education

Attn.: State Director, School Food Services Division
65 South Front Street, Room 713
Columbus, OH 43215-4183
Phone: 614-466-2945
Fax: 614-752-7613
http://cns.ode.state.oh.us/

**Ohio Department of Human Services
Office of Child Support Enforcement**

30 East Broad Street, 31st Floor
Columbus, OH 43266-0423
Phone: 614-752-6561
Fax: 614-752-9760

U.S. Small Business Administration

1111 Superior Avenue
Cleveland, OH 44114-2507
Phone: 216-522-4180
Fax: 216-522-2038

To report suspected child abuse in Ohio, call any county Children's Services Board or the county Human Services Department. Contact district offices of the Human Services Department in Columbus, Cleveland, Cincinnati, Canton, or Toledo for appropriate referral.
State Home Page: http://www.state.oh.us/
State Child Care Home Page: http://www.state.oh.us/odhs/cdc/index.htm

Oklahoma

**Oklahoma Department of Human Services
Division of Child Care**

Sequoyah Memorial Office Building
P.O. Box 25352
Oklahoma City, OK 73125-0352
Phone: 405-521-3561
Fax: 405-522-2564

**Head Start–State Collaboration Office
Oklahoma Association of Community Action Agencies (OACAA)**

2915 Classen, Suite 215
Oklahoma City, OK 73106
Phone: 405-524-4124
Fax: 405-524-0863
http://www.okacaa.org/headstart/state.html

**Department of Human Services
Office of Child Care**

Sequoyah Memorial Office Building
P.O. Box 25352
Oklahoma City, OK 73125-0352
Phone: 405-521-3561
Fax: 405-522-2564
http://okdhs.org/childcare/ProviderInfo/provinfo_licensing.htm

Child Care Resource Center

18 North Norwood
Tulsa, OK 74115
Phone: 918-834-2273
Fax: 918-834-9339
http://www.ccrctulsa.org/

Oklahoma Department of Education

Attn.: State Director, Child Nutrition Section
2500 North Lincoln Boulevard, Room 310
Oklahoma City, OK 73105-4599
Phone: 405-521-3327
Fax: 405-521-2239
http://sde.state.ok.us/pro/nut.html

Oklahoma Department of Human Services
Child Support Enforcement Division

P.O. Box 53552
Oklahoma City, OK 73152
Phone: 405-522-5871
Fax: 405-522-2753

U.S. Small Business Administration

210 Park Avenue, Suite 1300
Oklahoma City, OK 73102
Phone: 405-231-5521
Fax: 405-231-4876

_____

To report suspected child abuse in Oklahoma,
call 1-800-522-3511.
State Home Page: http://www.state.ok.us/
State Child Care Home Page: http://okdhs.org/
childcare/

Oregon

Oregon Department of Employment
Child Care Division

875 Union Street NE
Salem, OR 97311
Phone: 503-947-1400
Fax: 503-947-1428

Oregon Department of Education
Head Start Collaboration Office
Public Service Building

255 Capitol Street NE
Salem, OR 97310-0203
Phone: 503-378-5585 x 662
Fax: 503-373-7968
http://www.ode.state.or.us/stusvc/earlychild/

Employment Department
Child Care Division

875 Union Street NE
Salem, OR 97311
Phone: 503-947-1400
Fax: 503-947-1428
http://findit.emp.state.or.us/childcare/rules.cfm

Oregon Child Care Resource and Referral Network

1828 23rd Street SE
Salem, OR 97302
Phone: 503-375-2644
Fax: 503-399-9858
http://www.open.org/~occrrn/

Oregon Department of Education

Attn.: State Director, Child Nutrition and Food
Distribution
Public Services Building

255 Capitol Street NE
Salem, OR 97310-0203
Phone: 503-378-3579
Fax: 503-378-5258
http://www.ode.state.or.us/stusvc/Nutrition/

Oregon Department of Human Resources
Children, Adults and Family Services
Oregon Child Support Program

500 Summer Street NE
Salem, OR 97310-1013
Phone: 503-945-5600
Fax: 503-373-7032
http://www.afs.hr.state.or.us/childsupp.html

U.S. Small Business Administration

1515 SW 5th Avenue, Suite 1050
Portland, OR 97201-5494
Phone: 503-326-2682
Fax: 503-326-2808

_____

To report suspected child abuse in Oregon,
call 1-800-854-3508.
State Home Page: http://www.state.or.us/
State Child Care Home Page: http://
findit.emp.state.or.us/childcare/

Pennsylvania

Pennsylvania Department of Public Welfare
Office of Children, Youth, and Families

Box 2675
Harrisburg, PA 17105-2675
Phone: 717-783-3856
Fax: 717-787-1529
http://www.dpw.state.pa.us/ocyf/dpwocyf.asp

Pennsylvania Head Start–State Collaboration Office
Center for Schools and Communities

1300 Market Street, Suite 12
Lemoyne, PA 17043
Phone: 717-763-1661
Fax: 717-763-2083
http://www.center-school.org/comm_fam/hsscp/
index.html

Department of Public Welfare,
Bureau of Child Day Care
Office of Children, Youth, and Families

Bertolino Building, 4th Floor
P.O. Box 2675
Harrisburg, PA 17105-2675
Phone: 717-787-8691
Fax: 717-787-1529
http://www.dpw.state.pa.us/ocyf/childcarewks/
ccwreqccp.asp

Pennsylvania Department of Education

Attn.: State Director, Division of Food and
Nutrition
333 Market Street, 4th Floor
Harrisburg, PA 17126-0333
Phone: 717-787-7698
Fax: 717-783-6566
http://www.pde.psu.edu/nutrition/adult.html

Pennsylvania Department of Public Welfare
Bureau of Child Support Enforcement

P.O. Box 8018
Harrisburg, PA 17105
Phone: 717-783-5441
Fax: 717-772-4936

U.S. Small Business Administration

900 Market Street, 5th Floor
Philadelphia, PA 19107
Phone: 215-580-2722
Fax: 215-580-2762

———

To report suspected child abuse in Pennsylvania,
call 1-800-932-0313.
State Home Page: http://www.state.pa.us/
State Child Care Home Page: http://
www.dpw.state.pa.us/ocyf/ocyfdc.asp

Puerto Rico

Puerto Rico Department of the Family
Administration for Families and Children,
Child Care and Development Program

Avenida Ponce de Leon, PDA.2, San Juan
Apartado 15091
San Juan, PR 00902-5091
Phone: 787-722-8157
Fax: 787-721-6366

Puerto Rico Head Start–State Collaboration Office
Governor's Office
La Fortaleza

P.O. Box 902-0082
San Juan, PR 00902-0082
Phone: 787-721-7000
Fax: 787-721-5336

Department of Family Licensing Office

P.O. Box 11398
Santurce, PR 00910
Phone: 787-724-0772
Fax: 787-724-0767

Puerto Rico Department of Education

Attn.: State Director, Food and Nutrition Services
Teniente Cesar Gonzalez

P.O. Box 190759
San Juan, PR 00919-0759
Phone: 787-754-0790
Fax: 787-753-8155

Puerto Rico Department of Social Services
Administration for Child Support

P.O. Box 3349
San Juan, PR 00902
Phone: 787-767-1886
Fax: 787-282-8324

U.S. Small Business Administration
Puerto Rico and Virgin Islands District Office

252 Ponce De Leon Avenue, Suite 201
Hato Rey, PR 00918
Phone: 787-766-5572
Fax: 787-766-5309

———

To report suspected child abuse in Puerto Rico, call
787-724-7474 (Office of Family Administration).
State Home Page: http://fortaleza.govpr.org
State Child Care Home Page: http://
fortaleza.govpr.org/gobierno/familia1.htm

Rhode Island

Rhode Island Department of Human Services

Louis Pasteur Building, #57
600 New London Avenue
Cranston, RI 02920
Phone: 401-462-3415
Fax: 401-462-6878

Rhode Island Head Start–State Collaboration Office
Department of Human Services

600 New London Avenue
Cranston, RI 02920
Phone: 401-462-3071
Fax: 401-462-6878

Rhode Island Department of Children, Youth, and
Families Day Care Licensing Unit

101 Friendship Street
Providence, RI 02903
Phone: 401-528-3624
Fax: 401-528-3650
http://www.dcyf.state.ri.us/licensing.htm

Options for Working Parents

30 Exchange Terrace
Providence, RI 02903
Phone: 401-272-7510
Fax: 401-751-2434

Rhode Island Department of Education

Attn.: State Director, Office of
Integrated Social Services
Shepard Building
255 Westminster Street, Room 600
Providence, RI 02903-3400
Phone: 401-222-4600
Fax: 401-222-4979

**Rhode Island Department of Administration
Division of Taxation–Child Support Enforcement**

77 Dorrance Street
Providence, RI 09203
Phone: 401-222-2847
Fax: 401-222-2887

U.S. Small Business Administration

380 Westminster Street
Providence, RI 02903
Phone: 401-528-4561
Fax: 401-528-4539

To report suspected child abuse in Rhode Island,
call 1-800-RI-CHILD (1-800-742-4453).
State Home Page: http://www.state.ri.us/
State Child Care Home Page: http://
www.dhs.state.ri.us/

South Carolina

**South Carolina Department of
Health and Human Services
Bureau of Community Services,
Child Care and Development Services**

P.O. Box 8206
1801 Main Street, 8th Floor
Columbia, SC 29202-8206
Phone: 803-898-2570
Fax: 803-898-4510

**South Carolina Department of
Health and Human Services
South Carolina Head Start–State
Collaboration Office**

1801 Main Street, 10th Floor
Columbia, SC 29201
Phone: 803-898-2556
Fax: 803-253-4513

**Department of Social Services
Division of Child Day Care Licensing**

P.O. Box 1520
Room 520
Columbia, SC 29202-1520
Phone: 803-898-7345
Fax: 803-898-7179
http://www.state.sc.us/dss/cdclrs/index.html

**South Carolina Child Care Resources
Interfaith Community Services**

P.O. Box 11570
Columbia, SC 29211-1570
Phone: 803-252-8391
Fax: 803-799-1572

South Carolina Department of Social Services

Attn.: State Director, Food Services Operations
1535 Confederate Avenue, Room 601
P.O. Box 1520
Columbia, SC 29201-1520
Phone: 803-734-9500
Fax: 803-734-9515

**South Carolina Department of Social Services
Child Support Enforcement Division**

P.O. Box 1469
Columbia, SC 29202-1469
Phone: 803-737-5870
Fax: 803-737-6032

U.S. Small Business Administration

1835 Assembly Street, Room 358
Columbia, SC 29201
Phone: 803-765-5377
Fax: 803-765-5962

To report suspected child abuse in South Carolina,
call the Regional Office of the Department of Social
Services.
State Home Page: http://www.myscgov.com/
State Child Care Home Page: http://
www.dhhs.state.sc.us/FAQ/child_care.htm

South Dakota

**South Dakota Department of Social Services
Child Care Services**

700 Governors Drive
Pierre, SD 57501-2291
Phone: 605-773-4766
Fax: 605-773-6834

**South Dakota Department of
Education and Cultural Affairs
Head Start–State Collaboration Office**

700 Governors Drive
Pierre, SD 57501-2291
Phone: 605-773-4640
Fax: 605-773-6846
http://www.state.sd.us/deca/DESR/Childhood/
headstart.htm

Department of Social Services
Child Care Services
Kneip Building

700 Governors Drive
Pierre, SD 57501-2291
Phone: 605-773-4766
Fax: 605-773-7294
http://www.state.sd.us/social/CCS/Licensing%
20&%20Registration/licensing2.htm

South Dakota State University (SDSU)
Family Resource Network

Box 2218-HDCFS/SDSU
Brookings, SD 57007
Phone: 605-688-5730

South Dakota Department of
Education and Cultural Affairs

Attn.: State Director, Child and Adult Nutrition
Services
700 Governors Drive
Pierre, SD 57501-2291
Phone: 605-773-3413
Fax: 605-773-6846
http://www.state.sd.us/deca/compser/chn.htm

South Dakota Department of Social Services
Office of Child Support Enforcement

700 Governors Drive
Pierre, SD 57501-2291
Phone: 605-773-3641
Fax: 605-773-6834
http://www.state.sd.us/social/cse/index.htm

U.S. Small Business Administration

110 South Phillips Avenue
Sioux Falls, SD 57102
Phone: 605-330-4231
Fax: 605-330-4215

To report suspected child abuse in South Dakota,
call the local Department of Social Services office
or a local law enforcement agency.
State Home Page: http://www.state.sd.us/
State Child Care Home Page: http://
www.state.sd.us/state/executive/social/
CCS/CCShome.htm

Tennessee

Tennessee Department of Human Services
Child Care Services

Citizens Plaza, 14th Floor
400 Deaderick Street
Nashville, TN 37248-9600
Phone: 615-313-4778
Fax: 615-532-9956

Tennessee Department of Education,
Office of School-Based Support Services
Head Start–State Collaboration Office

Andrew Johnson Tower
710 James Robertson Parkway
Nashville, TN 37243-0375
Phone: 615-741-4849
Fax: 615-532-4899

Department of Human Services
Child Care Services Unit
Citizens Plaza

400 Deaderick Street
Nashville, TN 37248-9800
Phone: 615-313-4778
Fax: 615-532-9956

Tennessee Department of Human Services
Child Care Resource and Referral Center

400 Deaderick Street, 14th Floor
Nashville, TN 37248-9810
Phone: 615-313-4820

Tennessee Department of Human Services

Attn.: State Director, Adult and
Community Programs
Citizens Plaza Building, 15th Floor
400 Deaderick Street
Nashville, TN 37248-9500
Phone: 615-313-4749
Fax: 615-532-9956

Tennessee Department of Human Services
Child Support Services

Citizens Plaza Building, 12th Floor
400 Deaderick Street
Nashville, TN 37248-7400
Phone: 615-313-4879
Fax: 615-741-4165

U.S. Small Business Administration

50 Vantage Way, Suite 201
Nashville, TN 37228-1500
Phone: 615-736-5881
Fax: 615-736-7232

To report suspected child abuse in Tennessee, call any county's 24-hour hotline.
State Home Page: http://www.state.tn.us/
State Child Care Home Page: http://www.state.tn.us/humanserv/childcare.htm

Texas

Texas Workforce Commission

101 East 15th Street, Suite 434T
Austin, TX 78778-0001
Phone: 512-936-3141
Fax: 512-936-3223
http://www.twc.state.tx.us/svcs/childcare/ccinfo.html

Texas Head Start–State Collaboration Office
Office of the Governor

P.O. Box 12428
Austin, TX 78711
Phone: 512-936-4059
Fax: 512-463-7392
http://www.governor.state.tx.us/the_office/head_start/main.htm

Department of Protective and Regulatory Services
Child Care Licensing

P.O. Box 149030
M.C. E-550
Austin, TX 78714-9030
Toll Free: 800-862-5252 or 512-438-3267
Fax: 512-438-3848
http://www.tdprs.state.tx.us/Child_Care/

Texas Association of Child Care
Resource and Referral Agencies

1500 W. University Avenue, Suite 105
Georgetown, TX 78628
Phone: 512-868-0552
Fax: 512-868-5743
http://www.taccrra.org

Texas Department of Human Services

Attn.: State Director, Client Self-Support Services
1106 Clayton Lane, Suite 217E
P.O. Box 149030
Austin, TX 78714-9030
Phone: 512-483-3941
Fax: 512-467-5855
http://www.dhs.state.tx.us/programs/snp/index.html

Texas Office of the Attorney General
Child Support Division

P.O. Box 12017
Austin, TX 78711-2017

Phone: 512-460-6000
Fax: 512-460-6028
http://www.oag.state.tx.us/child/mainchil.htm

U.S. Small Business Administration

4300 Amon Carter Boulevard, Suite 108
Dallas/Ft.Worth, TX 76155
Phone: 817-684-6581
Fax: 817-684-6588

To report suspected child abuse in Texas, call 1-800-252-5400.
State Home Page: http://www.state.tx.us/
State Child Care Home Page: http://www.twc.state.tx.us/svcs/childcare/ccinfo.html

Utah

Utah Department of Workforce Services
Policy and Program Unit

1385 S. State Street
Salt Lake City, UT 84115
Phone: 801-468-0123
Fax: 801-468-0160

Utah Department of Health Child, Adolescent, and
School Health Programs (CASH)
Head Start–State Collaboration Office

P.O. Box 142001
Salt Lake City, UT 84114-2001
Phone: 801-538-9312
Fax: 801-538-9409
http://www.hlunix.hl.state.ut.us/cfhs/mch/cash/headstart.html

Department of Health
Bureau of Licensing
Child Care Unit

P.O. Box 142003
Salt Lake City, UT 84114-2003
Phone: 801-538-9299
Fax: 801-538-9259
http://www.health.state.ut.us/hsi/hfl/index.html

Family Connections Resource and Referral Center
Utah Valley State College

800 West 1200 South
Orem, UT 84058
Phone: 801-222-8220

Utah State Office of Education

Attn.: State Director, Child Nutrition Programs
250 East 500 South Street
Salt Lake City, UT 84111-3284
Phone: 801-538-7513
Fax: 801-538-7883
http://www.usoe.k12.ut.us/cnp/index.htm

Utah Department of Human Services
Bureau of Child Support Services

P.O. Box 45011
515 East 100 South
Salt Lake City, UT 84145-0011
Phone: 801-536-8911
Fax: 801-536-8509

U.S. Small Business Administration

125 South State Street, Room 2231
Salt Lake City, Utah 84138
Phone: 801-524-3209
Fax: 801-524-4160 or 4410

———

To report suspected child abuse in Utah,
call 801-538-4377 (not toll free).
State Home Page: http://www.state.ut.us/
State Child Care Home Page: http://
occ.dws.state.ut.us/

Vermont

Vermont Department of Social and
Rehabilitation Services
Agency for Human Services
Child Care Services Division

103 South Main Street, 2nd Floor
Waterbury, VT 05671-2401
Phone: 802-241-3110
Fax: 802-241-1220
http://www.state.vt.us/srs/childcare/index.htm

Vermont Head Start–State Collaboration Office
Agency of Human Services

103 South Main Street
Waterbury, VT 05671-0204
Phone: 802-241-2705
Fax: 802-241-2979

Department of Social Rehabilitation Services
Child Care Services Division
Child Care Licensing Unit

103 South Main Street
Waterbury, VT 05671-2901
Phone: 802-241-2158 or 3110
Fax: 802-241-1220
http://www.state.vt.us/srs/childcare/licensing/
license.htm

Vermont Association of Child Care
Resource and Referral Agencies

P.O. Box 542
Hinesburg, VT 05461
Phone: 802-482-4400
Fax: 802-482-5446

Vermont Department of Education

Attn.: State Director, Child Nutrition Programs
120 State Street
Montpelier, VT 05602-2702
Phone: 802-828-5154
Fax: 802-828-5107
http://www.state.vt.us/educ/nutrition/

Vermont Office of Child Support

103 South Main Street
Waterbury, VT 05671-1901
Phone: 802-241-2319
Fax: 802-244-1483
http://www.osc.state.vt.us/

U.S. Small Business Administration

87 State Street
Montpelier, VT 05602
Phone: 802-828-4422
Fax: 802-828-4485

———

To report suspected child abuse in Vermont,
call 802-241-2131 (not toll free).
State Home Page: http://www.state.vt.us/
State Child Care Home Page: http://
www.state.vt.us/srs/childcare/index.htm

Virgin Islands

Virgin Islands Department of Human Services
Knud Hansen Complex Building A

1303 Hospital Ground
Charlotte Amalie, St. Thomas, VI 00802
Phone: 340-774-0930
Fax: 340-774-3466

Department of Human Services
Child Care Licensing

3011 Golden Rock
Christiansted, St. Croix
U.S. Virgin Islands 00820-4355
Phone: 340-773-2323
Fax: 340-773-6121

Department of Education

Attn.: State Director, Child Nutrition Programs
44-46 Kongens Gade
Charlotte Amalie, St. Thomas, VI 00802
Phone: 340-774-9373
Fax: 340-774-9705

Virgin Islands Department of Justice
Paternity and Child Support Division

GERS Building, 2nd Floor
48B-50C Kronprindsens Gade
St. Thomas, VI 00802
Phone: 340-774-4339
Fax: 340-774-9710

To report suspected child abuse in the Virgin Islands, call 1-800-422-4453 (ChildHelp USA). State Home Page: http://www.usvi.org/

Virginia

Virginia Department of Social Services
Child Day Care

730 E. Broad Street
Richmond, VA 23219-1849
Phone: 804-692-1298
Fax: 804-692-2209
http://www.dss.state.va.us/family/childcare.html

Virginia Department of Social Services
Child Day Care Programs
Head Start–State Collaboration Office

730 East Broad Street, 2nd Floor
Richmond, VA 23219-1849
Phone: 804-692-0935
Fax: 804-786-9610
http://www.dss.state.va.us/family/
headstartco.html

Department of Social Services
Division of Licensing Programs

730 E. Broad Street, 7th Floor
Richmond, VA 23219-1849
Phone: 804-692-1787 or 1-800-543-7545
Fax: 804-692-2370
http://www.dss.state.va.us/division/license/

Council of Community Services

P.O. Box 598
Roanoke, VA 24004
Phone: 540-985-0131
Fax: 540-982-2935

Virginia Department of Social Services
Division of Child Support Enforcement

730 East Broad Street
Richmond, VA 23219
Phone: 804-692-1501
Fax: 804-692-1543
http://www.dss.state.va.us/division/childsupp/

U.S. Small Business Administration

Federal Building, Suite 1150
400 North 8th Street, Box 10126
Richmond, VA 23240-0126
Phone: 804-771-2400
Fax: 804-771-2764

To report suspected child abuse in Virginia, call 1-800-552-7096.
State Home Page: http://www.state.va.us/

State Child Care Home Page: http://www.dss.state.va.us/family/childcare.html

Washington

Division of Child Care and Early Learning
Economic Services Administration
Department of Social and Health Services

P.O. Box 45480
Olympia, WA 98504
Phone: 360-413-3209
Fax: 360-413-3482

Head Start–State Collaboration Project
Washington State Department of
Social and Health Services,
Economic Services Administration
Division of Child Care and Early Learning

P.O. Box 45480
Olympia, WA 98504

Department of Social and Health Services
Office of Child Care Policy

P.O. Box 45700
Olympia, WA 98504
Phone: 360-902-8039
Fax: 360-902-7903
http://www.wa.gov/dshs/occp/license.html

Washington State Child Care
Resource and Referral Network

917 Pacific Avenue, Suite 600
Tacoma, WA 98402-4421
Phone: 253-383-1735
Alt. Phone: 800-446-1114
Fax: 253-572-2599
http://www.childcarenet.org/

Washington Office of Superintendent of
Public Instruction

Attn.: State Director, Child Nutrition Section
Old Capitol Building, 600 South Washington Street
P.O. Box 47200
Olympia, WA 98504-7200
Phone: 360-753-3580
Fax: 360-664-9397
http://www.k12.wa.us/ChildNutrition/

Washington DSHS
Division of Child Support

P.O. Box 9162
Olympia, WA 98507-9162
Phone: 360-586-3520
Fax: 360-586-3274

U.S. Small Business Administration

1200 6th Avenue, Suite 1805
Seattle, WA 98101-1128
Phone: 206-553-5676
Fax: 206-553-2872

To report suspected child abuse in Washington, call 1-866-End Harm.
State Home Page: http://access.wa.gov/
State Child Care Home Page: http://www.wa.gov/dshs/occp/index.html

West Virginia

**West Virginia Department of
Health and Human Resources
Bureau for Children and Families
Office of Social Services, Division of
Planning Services**

350 Capitol Street, Room 691
Charleston, WV 25301-3700
Phone: 304-558-0938
Fax: 304-558-8800

**Governor's Cabinet on Children and Families
Head Start–State Collaboration Office**

1900 Kanawha Boulevard East
Capitol Complex, Building 5, Room 218
Charleston, WV 25305
Phone: 304-558-4638
Fax: 304-558-0596

**Department of Health and Human Resources
Day Care Licensing**

P.O. Box 2590
Fairmont, WV 26555-2590
Phone: 304-363-3261
Fax: 304-367-2729
http://www.wvdhhr.org/oss/childcare/licensing.htm
http://www.daycare.com/westvirginia/

River Valley Child Development Services

2850 5th Avenue
Huntington, WV 25702
Phone: 304-523-3417

West Virginia Department of Education

Attn.: State Director, Office of Child Nutrition
Building 6, Room B-248
1900 Kanawha Boulevard East
Charleston, WV 25305-0330
Phone: 304-558-2708
Fax: 304-558-1149

**West Virginia Department of
Health and Human Resources
Bureau of Child Support Enforcement**

350 Capitol Street, Room 147
Charleston, WV 25305-3703
Phone: 304-558-3780
Fax: 304-558-4092
http://www.wvdhhr.org/bcse/

U.S. Small Business Administration

320 West Pike Street, Suite 330
Clarksburg, WV 26301
Phone: 304-623-5631
Fax: 304-623-4269

To report suspected child abuse in West Virginia, call 1-800-352-6513.
State Home Page: http://www.state.wv.us/
State Child Care Home Page: http://www.wvdhhr.org/oss/childcare/

Wisconsin

**Wisconsin Department of Workforce Development
Office of Child Care**

201 E. Washington Avenue, Room 171
P.O. Box 7935
Madison, WI 53707-7935
Phone: 608-267-3708
Fax: 608-261-6968
http://www.dwd.state.wi.us/dws/programs/childcare/default.htm

**Wisconsin Department of Workforce Development
Office of Child Care
Head Start–State Collaboration Office**

201 E. Washington Avenue
Madison, WI 53707-7935
Phone: 608-261-4596
Fax: 608-267-3240

**Division of Children and Family Services
Bureau of Regulation and Licensing**

1 West Wilson Street
P.O. Box 8916
Madison, WI 53708-8916
Phone: 608-266-9314
Fax: 608-267-7252
http://www.dhfs.state.wi.us/rl_dcfs/index.htm

**Wisconsin Child Care Resource and
Referral Network, Inc.**

519 W. Wisconsin Avenue
Appleton, WI 54911
Phone: 920-734-1739
Fax: 920-734-3887
http://www.wisconsinccrr.org/

Wisconsin Department of Public Instruction

Attn.: State Director, Food and Nutrition Services
125 South Webster Street
P.O. Box 7841
Madison, WI 53707-7841
Phone: 608-267-9121
Fax: 608-267-0363
http://www.dpi.state.wi.us/dpi/dfm/fns/

Wisconsin Division of Economic Support
Bureau of Child Support

P.O. Box 7935
Madison, WI 53707-7935
Phone: 608-266-9909
Fax: 608-267-2824

U.S. Small Business Administration

310 W. Wisconsin Avenue, Room 400
Milwaukee, WI 53203
Phone: 414-297-3941
Fax: 414-297-1377

———

To report suspected child abuse in Wisconsin, call the county Department of Social or Human Services or the local sheriff or police department.
State Home Page: http://www.wisconsin.gov/state/home/
State Child Care Home Page: http://www.dwd.state.wi.us/des/childcare/

Wyoming

Wyoming Department of Family Services

Hathaway Building, Room 372
2300 Capitol Avenue
Cheyenne, WY 82002-0490
Phone: 307-777-6848
Fax: 307-777-7747
http://dfsweb.state.wy.us/

Head Start–State Collaboration Office

1465 N. 4th Street, Suite 111
Laramie, WY 82072
Phone: 307-766-2452
Fax: 307-721-2084
http://wind.uwyo.edu/headstart/

Department of Family Services
Division of Juvenile Services

Hathaway Building, Room 343
2300 Capitol Avenue
Cheyenne, WY 82002-0490
Phone: 307-777-6285
Fax: 307-777-3659

Child Care Finder

c/o Children and Nutrition Services
P.O. Box 2455
800 Werner Court, Suite 185
Casper, WY 82602
Phone: 307-235-7921
Toll Free: 1-800-583-6129
Fax: 307-266-4410
http://www.childrens-nutrition.com/page4.html

Wyoming Department of Education

Attn.: State Director, Health and Safety Programs
Hathaway Building, 2nd Floor
2300 Capitol Avenue
Cheyenne, WY 82002-0050
Phone: 307-777-6282
Fax: 307-777-6234
http://www.k12.wy.us/hsandn/index.html

Wyoming Department of Family Services
Child Support Enforcement Program

Hathaway Building, Room 361
2300 Capitol Avenue
Cheyenne, WY 82002-0710
Phone: 307-777-3695
Fax: 307-777-3693

U.S. Small Business Administration
Wyoming District Office

100 East B Street,
Room 4001, Federal Building
P.O. Box 2839
Casper, WY 82602
Phone: 307-261-6500
Toll Free: 1-800-776-9144, Ext. 1
TTY/TDD: 307-261-6527
Fax: 307-261-6535

———

To report suspected child abuse in Wyoming, call 1-800-457-3659.
State Home Page: http://www.state.wy.us/
State Child Care Home Page: http://dfsweb.state.wy.us/childcare/toc.htm

References

Ainsworth, M. D. S. (1974). Infant-mother attachment and social development: Socialization as a product of reciprocal responsiveness to signals. In M. Edwards (Ed.), *The integration of the child into the social work.* Cambridge: Cambridge University Press.

Ausubel, D. P. (1959). *Theory and problems of child development.* New York: Grune & Stratton.Brand, M., & Garcia-Tunon, A. (1999, spring). Welcom, bienvenido, and ways to make second-language learners feel welcome in Head Start. *Children and Families, 18*(2), 16–18.

Division of Instructional Services, Early Childhood Team (1997). *The North Carolina guide for the early years.* Raleigh: North Carolina Dept. of Public Instruction.

Garvey, C. (1977). Play with language and speech. In S. Ervin-Tripp & C. Mitchell-Kerman (Eds.), *Child discourse.* New York: Academic Press.

Gestwicki, C. (1999). *Developmentally appropriate practice: Curriculum and development in early education* (2nd ed.). Clifton Park, NY: Delmar Learning.

Gonzales-Mena, J., & Eyer, D. W. (1997). Multicultural issues in childcare (2nd ed.). Mountain View, CA: Mayfield.

Greenman, J. (1988). *Caring spaces, learning places: Children's environments that work.* Redmond, WA: Exchange Press.

Hull, K., Goldhaber, J., & Capone, A. (2002). *Opening doors: An introduction to inclusive early childhood education.* Boston: Houghton Mifflin.

Moore, G. T. (1997, January). Houses and their resource-rich activity pockets. *Child Care Information Exchange, 113,* 15–20.

Rheingold, H. L., & Eckerman, C. O. (1971). Departures from the mother. In H. R. Schaffer (Ed.), *The origins of human social relations* (pp. 180–223). New York: Academic Press.

Smith, P., & Connolly, K. (1980). *The ecology of preschool behavior.* Cambridge: Cambridge University Press.

Sroufe, L. A., & Waters, E. (1977). Attachment as an organizational construct. *Child Development, 48,* 1184–1199.

Stern, D. (1977). *The first relationship: Infant and mother.* Cambridge, MA: Harvard University Press.

Index